Students and F

PHILLIPPS STUDIES
NO. 5

THE DISPERSAL OF
THE PHILLIPPS LIBRARY

THOMAS FITZROY FENWICK IN THE LIBRARY AT THIRLESTAINE HOUSE

THE DISPERSAL OF THE PHILLIPPS LIBRARY

BY

A. N. L. MUNBY

Fellow and Librarian
King's College
Cambridge

CAMBRIDGE
AT THE UNIVERSITY PRESS
1960

PUBLISHED BY
THE SYNDICS OF THE CAMBRIDGE UNIVERSITY PRESS
Bentley House, 200 Euston Road, London, N.W. 1
American Branch: 32 East 57th Street, New York 22, N.Y.

©

CAMBRIDGE UNIVERSITY PRESS
1960

Printed in Great Britain at the University Press, Cambridge
(Brooke Crutchley, University Printer)

CONTENTS

v

CONTENTS

PLATES

PREFACE

It was, I think, Macaulay who remarked that few readers were up with Sir Calidore when he cornered the Beast in Book VI of *The Faerie Queene*. I fear that those who have followed the fortunes of Sir Thomas Phillipps through the previous four volumes will experience a similar flagging of interest in this fifth and final instalment. Having killed off our hero at the end of volume four we are left with *Phillipps Studies* without Phillipps: *Hamlet* without the Prince of Denmark would be lively by comparison. It is true that the Baronet makes a short posthumous appearance in the first chapter, and that occasional inherited flashes of his spirit gleam fitfully in the temperament of his grandson, but these are small compensations to offset the comparatively humdrum nature of large tracts of the history of the library's dispersal. Nevertheless a process which has gone on continuously since 1886 and which has produced a sum approaching four hundred thousand pounds is not without its significance in the history of book-collecting.

Two years ago Mr L. J. Gorton and I in collaboration appealed to owners and custodians of Phillipps manuscripts to send us notes of them so that a tentative finding-list could be attached to this volume. The response has been gratifyingly large, so large that the finding-list has far outgrown its intended role as an appendix. While I have been completing my narrative history of the Phillipps Library Mr Gorton has shouldered the burden of recording the information which we have collected jointly relating to the present locations of the manuscripts, and this work, at present on cards in the Department of Manuscripts, British Museum, has already proved widely useful. It is still our intention to print it in due course, but a further short delay will serve only to improve it, the more so since the sorting out of the residue of the collection by Messrs Lionel and Philip Robinson is still far from complete. It will also benefit from production in a larger format than that of these *Studies*, and must be regarded as a separate publication.

To the finding-list will be attached certain other enumerative matter such as a list of manuscripts to which two distinct Phillipps numbers were allotted in error. I only regret having at this stage to postpone acknowledging the help of many librarians, archivists, scholars, book-collectors and booksellers who have been good enough to send contributions to the census of Phillipps manuscripts. The present volume therefore brings *Phillipps Studies* to its conclusion and I have printed at the end additions and corrections to the four previous volumes and a general index to the whole work, compiled by Mrs H. M. Nixon.

As the history of the library reaches modern times my indebtedness to other helpers grows heavier. In the first place I must express my warm gratitude to Messrs Lionel and Philip Robinson who have consistently aided and encouraged my labours and who have spent many hours producing information for me from their records. I am especially grateful to them for enabling me to write a full and frank account of the very recent events recorded in chapter VI and for reading and commenting upon the whole work in draft. The Fenwick Trustees and Mr E. J. Holloway of Walker, Martineau and Co., the Trustees' solicitors, have kindly read the final chapter in draft, and Mr Holloway has been good enough to make some valuable emendations. Parts of the same chapter were kindly read and approved by Mr Alan Fenwick, life-tenant of the Phillipps Library at the time of its sale to Messrs Robinson.

I am also grateful for help in recording several particular episodes. Mr Frederick B. Adams, Junior, kindly supplied information on the sales to John Pierpont Morgan I and II; Sir Chester Beatty was good enough to check my account of his purchases and those of his wife; the late Dr R. I. Best sent his delightful reminiscences of his visit to Thirlestaine House on behalf of the National Library of Ireland; Dr Dorothy Coveney and Mr J. W. Scott gave much help in unravelling the tangled history of the German manuscripts which should have passed to University College, London; Professor William A. Jackson sent me his file and other information relating to the projected participation of Harvard University Library in the purchase of the residue of the Phillipps Collection; Mr Walter Oakeshott supplied details of his astonishing discovery of Raleigh's commonplace book; and Mr Edwin Wolf 2nd amplified and amended my account of the transactions with Dr Rosenbach.

Mr Arthur Cole expounded to me the working of the Settled Land Acts, and on other points of detail I am indebted to Sir Harold Bell, Sir Sydney Cockerell, Mr Geoffrey Cumberlege, Mr H. G. Fletcher, Mr Alan Keen, Dr Eric Millar, and others whose aid is, I hope, acknowledged at the relevant passages in the text or foot-notes. I am also grateful to the editors of *The Book Collector* and *Het Boek* for allowing me to reproduce in chapters I and III certain material which had already appeared in their pages.

I am grateful once again to Mr George Rylands for reading the whole volume in typescript and for pointing out several stylistic infelicities, and to Mr J. C. T. Oates for casting his vigilant eye over the page proofs.

A. N. L. M.

King's College, Cambridge

1959

CHAPTER I

1819–1872

Plans for disposal of the library made in Phillipps's lifetime — first
Bodleian negotiation — the British Museum — the Welsh project —
Swansea — second attempt to come to terms with the University of
Oxford — Trusteeship of the British Museum — Llandovery and
Manorbier — correspondence with Disraeli — Phillipps's will — the
library passes to the Fenwicks.

The schemes which revolved in Phillipps's brain for the disposal of
his library were many and various, and were prompted by a whole
series of different motives. On several occasions the threat of
bankruptcy forced the collector to investigate the desperate
expedient of selling the whole or part of the library; at other times
the desire to safeguard the great collection against use by Roman
Catholics or by the hated Halliwell was the dominant factor; and
there was always present the wish to set up the library as an
endowed institution for literary research, in the use of which
successive generations of scholars would honour the name of its
founder. We have already referred to the intransigent perverseness
in negotiation which brought all these schemes to nothing.
Phillipps was neither temperamentally capable of giving freely, nor
was he even prepared to sell the books outright. Conditions,
always irksome and often impossible, were laid before trustees,
curators and governing bodies, conditions moreover which were
constantly changed with the mood of the potential donor, to the
despair of those friends of Letters who sought to persuade
reluctant colleagues that almost no price in money and vexation
was too high to pay to secure intact for posterity so magnificent
an heirloom as the Phillipps Library.

Since these projects bore no fruit the description of them must
not detain us overlong. As early as 1819 the collector made a will
in which he bequeathed his manuscripts relating to Wiltshire and

Oxfordshire to the Society of Antiquaries. In 1827, when more than usually hard pressed for money, he opened negotiations with Philip Bliss with a view to selling the collection to the University of Oxford. Bliss consulted Dean Gaisford and on 27 February replied that there was little hope of the University finding the money for such a substantial purchase. Nevertheless Phillipps corresponded on the subject with Bulkeley Bandinel, Bodley's Librarian, and in April 1828 sent him detailed proposals to be laid before the Curators.

Sir Thomas Phillipps being desirous of depositing his Collection of Manuscripts in a place of safety during his life time and preferring the Bodleian Library as being in his opinion more secure from fire than any other, as well as from a natural wish to enrich his own University, proposes to the Curators of the Bodleian Library the purchase of his Manuscripts.

The whole Collection has cost Sir Thomas Phillipps about Fifty Thousand Pounds but he is willing to part with them to his own University for Thirty Thousand Pounds, on conditions that the sole management of them during his life time shall be vested in the said Sir Thomas Phillipps.

2ndly That a room in the Bodleian Quadrangle shall be appropriated for their sole reception which shall not be connected or interfere with the other parts of the Bodleian Library.

3rdly That whatever books Sir Thomas Phillipps may wish to consult or to print, he shall be at liberty to have them in his own house either at Middle Hill or in London or wherever he may reside, except on the Continent, Sir T.P. always leaving a note in the library that such book or books are so taken out by him.

4thly That Sir T.P. shall have access at all hours to his own library & for that purpose a private key of all the doors leading to it shall be given to him, as well as the key of the library itself, but that it shall not be permitted him ever to enter it with candles or lamps.

5th That the Library shall be for ever kept entire and distinct from the other collections, under the name of "Bibliotheca Phillippica".

6th That no person or persons shall ever interfere in the management & arrangement of the said books, except one triennial visit of the Curators to see that the books are there.

7th That after Sir T.P.'s decease the Curators may remove the

Library into any other room in the Bodleian more conveniently situated for the Librarians, but that in all cases it shall be kept together & entire as the Collection of Sir T.P. under the title aforesaid.

8th That the Curators will give permission to let a flue be constructed for the admission of warm air, in the same manner as in the Bodleian Library itself.

9th That the Curators will permit the Manuscripts of the Meerman Collection already in the Bodleian to be incorporated with that portion of them in the Library of Sir T.P. it being his intention to restore that Collection to its original condition as far as lies in his power by future purchases.

In a letter of 12 May Bandinel reported that the Curators would not entertain these conditions. 'In all *purchases*', he wrote, 'they must consider themselves *free*; in the case of donations, the will of the donor must undoubtedly be gratefully consulted and followed; but when we purchase any books of whatsoever number, it is impossible for us to agree to any terms which would place them in a different state from the other parts of this library.' This refusal led Phillipps to approach the Trustees of the British Museum, who declined an offer of his manuscripts and coins on 11 November 1828. Nor was he more successful in 1830 in his attempt to sell to the Athenæum twelve thousand of his printed books for the sum of £6000, and the same year saw the failure of a plan to get raised in Parliament the question of the Government's purchase of his manuscripts for the nation. A second direct approach to the authorities of the British Museum resulted in a formal refusal on 10 January 1831 to buy the manuscripts for £60,000. Nevertheless in a draft will, mutilated but probably assignable to the year 1832, Phillipps made the following provision:

I do give all my Manuscripts to this Nation of Great Britain [he wrote] to be deposited in the British Museum, as, and by the Name of, the Phillipps Library of MSS., to be kept distinct from the other Collections there. And this I give, trusting that the Nation will have the liberality & generosity to pay my Debts both Mortgages, Bonds, Notes, & Bills of Exchange, and that the Nation will make a Provision of Eight or Ten thousand Pounds for my youngest daughter Katharine, who will otherwise have nothing.

During the 1830's Phillipps's financial position improved slightly, and, though he could hardly have been described as solvent, he did not again have to contemplate any measure so desperate as the sale of his entire collection, and no further negotiations about its ultimate fate took place until 1850. In this year Phillipps attended a meeting of the Cambrian Archaeological Association at Dolgelly at which he was reported to have made the following remarks:

Sir Thomas Phillipps took occasion to observe that he had noticed with regret the absence of public libraries in Wales, and that he intended to offer his own magnificent collection to be at some central place in the Principality.

The expression of this liberal intention encouraged the Borough of Swansea to stake its claim. The prime mover appears to have been the antiquary George Grant Francis (1814–82), Honorary Librarian of the Royal Institution of South Wales at Swansea, the Council of which lost no time in forwarding a resolution to Phillipps urging the suitability of the Institution as a place of deposit for the library. On 18 October 1850 the matter was brought before Swansea Borough Council, which transmitted through the Mayor a resolution expressing the Corporation's wish to aid the project by any means in its power. Though Phillipps was flattered by the interest which his remarks had aroused he replied that in his view a site in Central Wales would be far more suitable; and his subsequent discovery that a laboratory was attached to the Swansea Institution provided a deterrent even more forcible than its remoteness from North Wales. His doubts were strengthened by a letter written on 27 October by John Williams of Llandovery asserting roundly that the Swansea Institution was 'nothing better than those commonly established for the improvement of mechanical knowledge'. In his reply to Williams on 30 October Phillipps suggested that the gentlemen of Wales should subscribe for the erection of a suitable building in Llandovery, but no steps were taken to organize such a sub-

4

scription. When Phillipps sought advice from the Welsh archaeo-
logist Harry Longueville Jones (1806–70) he received a decidedly
discouraging rejoinder.

I do not wish to underrate the intellect of Wales [Jones wrote from
Bangor on 8 January 1851] but I do know that great apathy exists as to
all that concerns literature, science, or the fine arts. I know of nothing
in which my fellow countrymen shew any energy except in mining,
drinking,—writing half-drunken rhymes for prizes at Eisteddfodau—
and embarking in polemical controversy without any theological
knowledge.

If the Collection of books were mine,—and if I had tolerably good
ground of confidence in my own life, I would wait a few years,—and
see how events developed themselves.

I have just seen Lampeter Library: it is exceedingly rich and choice:—
all the great books of reference:—all the fine editions:—few M.S.S.—
a librarian who visits it more or less daily:—the porter of the College
takes care of the books:—the students admitted to it *once a week*:—for
fear of reading *too much*? The roof was in such bad repair that a few
days before my visit the rain had come in in torrents, and the books
were in one class at that moment putting out on the floor to dry:—It is
a library comparatively unknown & unused—people in S. Wales, or
round Lampeter, *cannot* read.

Jones went on to say that, if Phillipps were really determined
to set his library up in Wales, the Royal Institution at Swansea
would be the best body to receive it. Certainly Phillipps should
avoid placing it in ecclesiastical hands, since, in the writer's view,
the secularization of the Church and its possessions could not be
long delayed. He urged, however, that such a precious collection would be safest in the British Museum, where indeed it
would be as or even more accessible to the majority of Welshmen,
for a journey from Aberystwyth to Bangor took two days as
opposed to only nine hours from Bangor or Swansea to London:
but on the whole he advised Phillipps to wait a few years before
coming to a decision. In spite of this gloomy picture, when
Phillipps made one of his numerous draft wills on 1 December
1862, after the failure of his long negotiations with Oxford and

his quarrel with Panizzi, he bequeathed his manuscripts to the Royal Institution at Swansea, 'not to be read or looked into by anybody for fifty years or more if James Orchard Halliwell should so long live'.

Negotiations with Oxford began in December 1852 and did not finally break down until March 1861. Sir Edmund Craster has charted their long and tortuous course,[1] involving the exchange of over one hundred and fifty letters between Phillipps and various representatives of the University, at first with Bandinel and then with H. O. Coxe, his successor as Bodley's Librarian, and with Benjamin Jowett during Coxe's government-sponsored mission to the Levant in 1857 in search of Greek manuscripts.[2] Phillipps sought at the outset to borrow a room in the Bodleian to house his manuscripts without committing himself to any firm promise that they would ultimately pass into the possession of the University. The Curators of the library made the most strenuous efforts to meet the collector's wishes, and when in October 1856 some empty book-cases arrived from Middle Hill hopes must have run high that manuscripts would shortly follow. No agreement however could be reached on the building to be set aside for the collection. At first Phillipps demanded the Ashmolean, stipulating that apartments in the basement should be allocated for his own residence. Rooms were provided, and a housekeeper employed from November 1859 to July 1860; and Coxe, who good-naturedly advanced part of her wages and expenses out of his own pocket, had the greatest difficulty in recovering the debt. The University however found it impossible to allot Phillipps the entire Ashmolean building, whereupon he demanded instead the whole of the Radcliffe Library. Part of this however had been promised by the authorities to Frederick William Hope (1797–1862) to house his benefaction to the University of his great collection of engraved portraits. Phillipps approached Hope to see

---

[1] *History of the Bodleian Library 1845–1945* (Oxford, 1952), pp. 83–7.
[2] See Coxe's *Report to Her Majesty's Government on the Greek Manuscripts yet remaining in the Libraries of the Levant* (1858).

whether he would surrender his share of the Radcliffe, but without success. 'If the Ashmolean', replied Hope with some reason on 22 November 1860, 'be unfit to place your collection in, it is also unfit for the reception of mine'.

On 23 February 1861 Phillipps proposed to Coxe that he himself should become Bodley's Librarian, with Coxe as his deputy, and that in return the manuscripts should come to Oxford. Since Coxe had himself been elected Librarian in the previous November he can hardly be blamed for thinking that Phillipps was not in earnest. At all events he did not comment upon this proposal in his reply, but instead asserted that if Phillipps would guarantee Oxford his collection he, Coxe, could guarantee Phillipps all the Radcliffe not allotted to the Hope portraits.

On 24 March Phillipps, in a formally phrased letter, complained that Coxe's desire for a 'guarantee...shews what you must think of me, & such an opinion must of course put an end to our correspondence'.

My dear Sir Thomas [replied Coxe]

I am very sorry that an unguarded expression of mine, should have turned you into being my 'obedt Servt' & the calling me 'Sir'—I had thought we had been too well acquainted too long, that it sh^d come to such a pass as this—However I hope you will find an asylum for your collection where they will be as well appreciated as they w^d have been with us—For 35 YEARS (I see by some letters of Bandinel) we have been trying to please you but without effect!!

Yours still (independent of the MSS) very sincerely

H. O. COXE

On 30 March Phillipps broke off negotiations in a letter which reproached Coxe with having allowed his personal dignity to stand in the way of the welfare of the library. 'If you had been really desirous to have my MSS. in Bodley', he wrote, 'you would have jumped at the proposition I made, of being Principal Librarian of Bodley, you of course becoming second.'

My own vanity [answered Coxe on 19 April] did not, I assure you, lead me to pass in silence your remarks about the headship of this place.

I simply thought you were in joke. The idea of a man of your rank and fortune offering himself for such a post, was what I could not entertain for a moment as a serious proposition.

It was perhaps fortunate that to Coxe's sweetness of disposition there was added a strong sense of the ridiculous, which, one hopes, sustained him throughout negotiations in which Phillipps appears at his most perverse. It is difficult to envisage any measures which he would have found wholly to his liking, and a reader of the correspondence might well doubt whether he had in fact any serious intention of the manuscripts' becoming the property of the University. Such doubts however are dispelled by the presence in the Phillipps papers of an indenture, dated 1853 but never executed. The document made over the Phillipps Library into the trusteeship of Sir Frederic Madden, who was to permit Phillipps to have the possession and enjoyment of it during his lifetime. On the collector's death Madden was to hand the library over to the Curators of the Bodleian, except for certain duplicate printed books which were to be distributed to University College, St John's College and Winchester College,[1] the last gift being conditional on the Warden and Fellows of Winchester providing a room for the books' reception on the same side of the cloisters as was situated the monument to the Baronet's kinsman, Owen Phillipps. The manuscripts were to remain locked and sealed in the Bodleian during the lifetime of James Orchard Halliwell and the key was to be retained by Sir Frederic Madden and only restored to the Librarian on Halliwell's death. If Madden predeceased Halliwell another trustee was to be appointed by his executors.

The final failure of the long negotiations with Oxford coincided with Phillipps's appointment as a Trustee of the British Museum, a measure engineered by Panizzi in an attempt to secure the Phillipps Library for that institution.[2] The goodwill engendered

[1] In 1855 and 1858 Phillipps made gifts of books to Winchester College, including Layard's *Nineveh and its Remains*.
[2] See *Phillipps Studies*, no. 4, pp. 103–9.

by this gesture soon evaporated, and within eighteen months the collector found himself at loggerheads with both the Principal Librarian and his own co-Trustees. Panizzi's negotiations had hardly begun before the collector announced that the 'mismanagement' of the British Museum had determined him to leave his collection elsewhere. At this juncture his thoughts turned once more towards Wales. As we have seen, he made a will on 1 December 1862 leaving the manuscripts to Swansea, but before long he conceived plans which involved other places in the Principality. On 6 November 1864 he wrote to ask Sir Erasmus Williams whether there was any likelihood of the gentlemen of Wales combining to meet the expense of fitting up the Old Palace of the bishops of St David's to receive his books. Soon afterwards the collector's fertile brain conceived a further scheme, no less than the purchase and repair of the ancient castle of Manorbier for the purpose. The site had double attractions; not only was it the birthplace of Giraldus Cambrensis, but it was also on the estate of the ancient family of Philipps of Picton Castle, from which Sir Thomas claimed descent. There were however difficulties. The Rev. J. H. A. Philipps of Picton was sympathetic and co-operative, but he was only a life-tenant of the estate and his trustees were reluctant to sell so historic a possession as the feudal stronghold of Manorbier, while Phillipps for his part scouted the idea of any form of lease of the property. After numerous letters had passed between the collector, his namesake and their respective solicitors, Phillipps finally abandoned his plan of placing the manuscripts at Manorbier in the summer of 1866.

In the meantime the possibility of establishing a library of printed books at Llandovery had been mooted, and to this end an iron room was erected at Phillipps's expense on land provided by Sir Erasmus Williams, who had sought to dissuade the collector from the Manorbier project. No sooner was the building completed however than it was badly damaged by a hurricane, and when it had been repaired, the appointment of a librarian seemed to be a necessary preliminary to the despatch of any books.

Phillipps felt that Sir Erasmus Williams and the inhabitants of Llandovery should pay for the erection of the librarian's house. This was not refused, but more information was solicited on the exact nature of the intended gift of books. Phillipps became discouraged and reverted to his Picton plan, not for the manuscripts, but for a library composed of his duplicate printed books. The iron room was dismantled and re-erected at Picton in February 1868, and at least two cases of books were despatched from Cheltenham. The galvanized iron structure however was found to be very damp and quite unsuitable for the housing of books. In August 1868 an estimate was prepared for replacing it at a cost of £1030 by a brick building, but nothing came of this plan, and at the end of the year the iron room was sold and the books returned to Thirlestaine House. Thus ended Phillipps's grandiose schemes for the literary enrichment of Wales, schemes which resulted in nothing but infinite trouble and vexation to two long-suffering gentlemen of the Principality.

If the library had been set up in Wales it was Phillipps's intention to endow it to the extent of six thousand pounds. After the failure of the Welsh plan the collector considered endowing it as a permanent public institution at Thirlestaine House. To this end he consulted the Chancellor of the Exchequer on how best such a legacy might be freed from the provisions of the Mortmain Act. At first Disraeli's reply was distinctly encouraging.

You are right in assuming [he wrote on 20 July 1867] that my father greatly respected you and your pursuits, & I have often heard him say, that he believed your name and collections would, some day, rank with those of the Bodleys and the Cracherodes.

I have inherited all that consideration for you, & I beg to assure you, on the part of H.M. Government, that they will be happy, in any way, to assist in forwarding your noble intentions.

If an act of Parl^t is necessary, I will myself undertake to carry it thro' the House of Commons.

Even after this auspicious beginning difficulties soon arose. The law-officers of the Crown naturally wished to know the details of the rules which Phillipps proposed to lay down for the management of the library and whether the funds for its upkeep were to be derived from landed or from personal property. The Baronet does not seem to have been prepared to answer such questions.

I do not see the necessity [he wrote to Disraeli on 3 December 1867] of consulting Legal Authorities, because I hope Parliament will *make a Law* for this particular Case. I offer to make my Library a permanent one to which the Public will have access under certain reservations & after a certain time & subject to such rules as I may lay down.

I conceive the Act may be framed thus

'Whereas Sir Thomas Phillipps is desirous that his Library of MSS & Printed Books shall not be dispersed for 500 years be it enacted that the said Library shall be so founded & established according to such Rules & Conditions as the said Sir Thomas Phillipps shall by will lay down for the Government of it & the said Library shall be supported by such Funds and Property as the said Sir Thomas Phillipps shall appoint notwithstanding any Act of Mortmain or any other Act limiting the disposition of Property now made or hereafter to be made.

And to encourage the foundation of the said Library it is hereby enacted that the said Library Houses & the Grounds attached to it shall be free from the Legacy Duties & Succession Duties & from all Property Taxes, & all Parochial Rates and Taxes whatsoever now or hereafter to be imposed upon any Property in Great Britain.'

I hope this will meet with your cordial approbation.

In a reply of great courtesy Disraeli made it clear that an Act of Parliament could not be sponsored on such terms as these.

Confidential

Dec. 17   DOWNING ST.   *1867*
                              S.W.

Dear Sir Thomas

I have given great consideration to your noble purpose respecting your Library & collections, & altho' I greatly sympathise with your intentions, I cannot hold out any prospect of my being able to induce Parliament to co-operate with you in the plan as, at present, proposed.

The House of Commons, I feel sure, will never recognise, & confirm, the trusts of a will not in existence at the time the Act passes, or wh:, if in existence, might be altered at any moment before your death. They will sanction no arrangement, I am persuaded, where the nature of the trusts, the conditions of donation, the site & extent of the houses & lands to be appropriated, & to be freed from the operation of the Mortmain Act, would be wholly unknown to Parliament.

I am sorry to throw difficulties in the way of plans of so elevated & commendable a character, as those on wh: you have done me the honor of consulting me, but I should still more regret to be the means of deceiving & disappointing you.

If I can be of any further use, command me at all times.

I trust you have recovered from your indisposition, & I remain, with great consideration,

faithfully yours,

B. DISRAELI

The decision not to write Phillipps a blank cheque to override the Statute of Mortmain both surprised and pained the collector. Mortmain legislation, as he pointed out in a further letter of 2 February 1868, was originally aimed at the monasteries and was designed to prevent the accumulation of property in the hands of monks 'banded together for the purpose of leading an idle and useless life'. It was indeed unfortunate if legislation of which he heartily approved could be applied to the endowment of a library and thus nullify his cherished schemes. The only solution, he felt, would be to leave the library to a foreign government, unfettered by or prepared to waive tiresome regulations relating to succession of property. Tentative overtures were made to the Prussian Government, overtures eagerly grasped at by Georg Heinrich Pertz, then head of the Royal Library at Berlin: but Phillipps, having excited his old friend with a glittering prospect, soon let the matter drop.

It would appear that during all these negotiations the will which Phillipps had made in 1862, bequeathing the library to Swansea, was still in force. It was not until 3 November 1868 that he revoked that bequest and produced the first draft of what was to be the final disposition. In a letter to his solicitor, Arthur Walker of 13 King's Road, Gray's Inn, he asked for a will to be drawn up leaving the library and Thirlestaine House to his daughter

Katharine Fenwick for her life and thereafter to her eldest son '& to such of his descendants in the male line as shall shew a natural love of reading Books in his Childhood & Boyhood'. Numerous conditions were attached to the bequest and if they were not complied with the contents of Thirlestaine House were to pass to the 'Public Library at Berlin'. A stream of codicils followed, as Phillipps vacillated in his choice of trustees, and in 1871 a new will was drawn by William Smith, a Winchcomb solicitor. 'If any difficulty should arise [he wrote to Smith on 27 September 1871] in the Settlement & preservation of my Library, I give my said Library to the King of Sweden to make a Public Library in Norway, such Library to be 10 or 15 miles from any Capital Town or Market Town, & such Library Building to consist entirely of Stone and Iron or Zinc without any Wood whatever, to avoid the risk of Fire.' The final draft of the will[1] was signed on 1 February 1872 only five days before the collector's death. Thirlestaine House and the library were duly placed in the hands of trustees for Katharine Fenwick, with a life interest for her third son Thomas FitzRoy after her. On 6 February Sir Thomas Phillipps took his final leave of his beloved manuscripts, having shelved and not solved the problem which had exercised his mind for over forty years. Incapable to the last of a grand and generous gesture of benefaction, which would have made certain the enrolling of his name in the company of such immortals as Bodley and Cotton, Sir Thomas devised instead an uncertain and precarious future for the mighty library the formation of which had obsessed his whole life, and for which he had sacrificed so much.[2]

[1] Printed in full in *Phillipps Studies*, no. 2, pp. 106–15.

[2] This chapter, with a few changes, appeared in *The Book Collector*, vol. v, no. 2, 1956, under the title of 'Sir Thomas Phillipps and the Disposal of his Library'.

CHAPTER II

1872-1885

John and Katharine Fenwick — the Trustees' predicament — irksome conditions governing inheritance of library — inadequate funds for its upkeep — fresh approaches to the British Museum — decision to exact a fee for use of library — resulting embarrassments — Thomas FitzRoy Fenwick takes charge — Settled Land Acts — application to Court of Chancery — authority to sell the manuscripts granted.

The will of Sir Thomas Phillipps imposed a heavy burden upon the life-tenants of Thirlestaine House. Katharine Fenwick and her husband John were nearly fifty years of age, and for the previous twenty years the latter had held the modest country living of Needwood in the diocese of Lichfield. Their son Thomas FitzRoy was sent to Christ Church, Oxford, in 1875, but at the time of his parents' succession to Thirlestaine he was too young to help them in their onerous duties. The peculiarities of the late Baronet's will received wide publicity, and, since the eyes of the world were upon them, the Trustees were the more anxious that the testator's directions should be carried out to the letter. Of the three original Trustees Richard Coxwell Rogers appears to have played a passive role, and the responsibility for decisions fell upon the Rev. John Haydon Cardew, and especially upon Samuel Higgs Gael, a local barrister of antiquarian tastes. As a first step the services of Edward Augustus Bond, Madden's successor as Keeper of Manuscripts at the British Museum and later Principal Librarian, were secured to make a valuation of the collection for probate. In the course of this operation he compiled a summary list of those manuscripts still uncatalogued at Phillipps's death, allotting to them the numbers 23838 to 26179. Gael drew up a careful memorandum for the guidance of the life-tenants, suggesting the manner in which they should comply with the conditions of the testator's will. Some of these were irksome in the

14

(*a*) The Rev. John Fenwick, who administered the Library from 1872 until about 1880. From a photograph taken in 1864.

(*b*) Alan Fenwick, Esq., the last life-tenant of the Library. From a photograph taken in 1940.

extreme, in particular his express injunction that any movement of books from room to room should be carried out by the Trustees or by the Fenwicks in person, and not by any stranger employed for the purpose. The printed books in the library were in considerable disorder at Phillipps's death, and their rearrangement was an urgent necessity if the house were to be rendered suitable for ordinary family life.

In the meantime the learned world continued to address numerous inquiries to the owners of the library, inquiries which John Fenwick made conscientious efforts to answer. The inheritance of a life-interest in a national institution proved to be no sinecure; nor were hard work and vexatious restrictions the only hardship which Phillipps's heirs suffered. More serious was the fact that seven-eighths of the Baronet's income had been derived from entailed estates which passed at his death to the Halliwells. Only about £1000 a year remained, from which several annuities had to be disbursed as a first charge, rates and taxes paid on the mansion of sixty rooms and other necessary liabilities met. In an affidavit filed in 1885 by Mrs Fenwick in the Court of Chancery it was recorded that her annual income under her father's will during the previous ten years had averaged less than £225, a trifling recompense for the assumption of crushing responsibilities.

To meet this situation several expedients were suggested. Mrs Everett Green[1] proposed that the library should be supported by a body of subscribers, who should have access to the books on certain days each week, and this suggestion had the influential support of Sir Thomas Duffus Hardy. Tentative approaches were made to the British Museum to see whether even at this stage some formula could not be found for the transference of the library to the nation, but the Museum's Trustees were disinclined to open negotiations. On 4 January 1876 Lord Acton suggested that a second attempt might be made.

[1] Mary Anne Everett Green (1818–95), *née* Wood, historian, dedicated her *Letters of Royal and Illustrious Ladies* (3 vols., 1846), to Phillipps, and compiled the early part of the index to his *Catalogus librorum manuscriptorum*.

I do not know [he wrote to John Fenwick] whether you will be of the opinion that Mr Bond might again in some little time move the question that was not entertained a year or two ago. He will tell you what a curious and fluctuating body the Standing Committee is. Two of the members who were among the least enterprising are there no more. It may happen that after the next election the board will present a considerably altered character, and will be more willing to assist in promoting such arrangements as may be satisfactory to Mrs Fenwick and to yourself.

It would be a relief to us [replied Fenwick on 11 January] if some arrangement could be made by the British Museum or others, by which a fixed income could be secured to us, for I daresay you are aware how *very* small an annual sum is left for keeping up this huge house and library. One plan I have thought of is, whether there could not be found a certain limited number of literary subscribers of high character who would subscribe say a total of £500 a year, for which they would have the privilege of consulting, collating or copying MSS. This would be more agreeable to us than the admission of the public so called and would ensure the admission of only bona fide literary persons.

In June 1877 John Fenwick was in correspondence with Bond again on the possibility of the sale of the collection to the nation. Lord Acton had consultations with the Master of the Rolls and the Phillipps Trustees were asked whether they would give their concurrence to the promotion of an Act of Parliament which would enable them to sell the library *en bloc* to the British Museum. Bond borrowed a copy of the catalogue of manuscripts to enable him to draw up a memorandum on the subject. But these preparations led to nothing. Fenwick's tentative valuation of £150,000 may have led the Treasury to discourage the Museum from proceeding: at all events no formal proposals were made on either side. Nor did any better fate attend the plan of raising a body of subscribers to the library, and instead it was decided that each scholar who came to consult a manuscript should pay a fee. For a few years the amount seems to have fluctuated but by 1880 a standard charge of one pound per day was fixed for access to the library. Manuscripts might be collated without any extra payment, but for complete transcripts or large extracts an additional sum was demanded which varied in accordance with the value of the manuscript.

Although this decision was just and inevitable the application of the rule involved the custodians of the collection in some unforeseen embarrassments. There is in fact no law of nature which directs that scholars should have free access to private libraries, but in this country by a liberal tradition of enlightened patronage owners of manuscripts, books and works of art have rarely denied the gratuitous use of their treasures to properly accredited students: and in the case of the Phillipps Library for nearly half a century it had been the owner's particular pride and joy to keep open house for visiting scholars. The monetary rewards of scholarship are usually meagre, and, at a period when the editor of a text might expect a fee of ten guineas from a university press, the imposition of a charge of a pound a day for the collation of a single manuscript represented a serious tax on learning. It was naturally repugnant to the gentlemanly feelings of John Fenwick to provide unknown correspondents with lengthy explanations of the peculiar circumstances which necessitated a demand for payment, yet in default of such explanations the motives of the Trustees were widely misunderstood, and a levy which was in fact dictated by dire necessity was at times attributed to illiberality or even to avarice.

It was certainly painful to John Fenwick to have to exact fees from fellow-parsons of antiquarian tastes and exiguous means, to argue with distinguished foreign savants who protested that they had been overcharged, to dun the irrepressible Dr Furnivall for outstanding arrears and to turn away visiting scholars with their work uncompleted because their funds were exhausted. Nor were all objections to payment based on pleas of poverty. 'I instinctively recoil from the thought of having to pay for access to God's word', wrote a Biblical scholar in 1888. The reasonable demand that strangers should procure letters of introduction from some official in a national library or in the case of foreigners from their embassy was also resented in certain quarters. 'I hardly know what you mean by way of "Reference",' wrote Ernest C. Richardson, Librarian of Hartford Theological Seminary, 'I have a U.S. passport.'

Distressing protests against the fee-system found their way into print. Ernst Ludwig in the preface to his edition of the *Carmina* of Commodianus[1] explained how he had been compelled to leave a manuscript uncollated, 'when the man who now owns this magnificent library sharply demanded from me more money than I could pay, so that I was prevented from seeing the book through the avarice of this insolent person who trades literature for money'.

The painful predicament in which John Fenwick found himself is well illustrated in an exchange of letters with the Rev. S. S. Lewis (1836–91), Fellow and Librarian of Corpus Christi College, Cambridge. In February 1874 Lewis wrote on behalf of a German scholar, Dr Zangemeister of Heidelberg, who required the collation of a manuscript. Fenwick suggested in reply that five pounds would be a suitable sum for the German to pay for this privilege, a figure which Lewis regarded as 'a very high charge, and one which will often be prohibitive'.

You will, I hope, forgive the freedom with which I have spoken [he added] but the marked courtesy which I (as every English man of letters) have always received from foreign Librarians, makes me anxious that they too should be treated with all reasonable favour, when *we* have the opportunity of shewing it.

Fenwick replied with a courteous letter explaining that the lack of endowment had necessitated the fee, which in the present instance he was prepared to reduce from five pounds to four.

In the case of extracts or copies [he wrote] by which of course a MS. is to a certain extent thereby depreciated in value, the charge will often be a very considerable one. This we are desirous the literary world should fully be made aware of, and you will be doing me a favour if you will make it generally known among your literary friends that everything has to be paid for.

[1] Leipzig, 1878, p. xi. I owe this reference to Dr F. J. E. Raby.

The phrasing was perhaps a little unfortunate; certainly the effect of this invitation to Lewis to publicize the charges was surprising and disagreeable. On 3 March 1874 Fenwick received the proof of a paragraph supplied by Lewis to the well-known literary journal *The Athenaeum*, together with a covering letter from the editor in which he was asked to state by return of post whether the proposed statement had his approval.

We are requested to state [ran the paragraph] that, for access to the Middlehill Library—so long known for the noble manuscripts and no less noble hospitality of the late Sir Thomas Phillipps,—a fee of 5l. is now asked by his son-in-law, the Rev. J. Fenwick, of Thirlestane [*sic*] House, Cheltenham.

Copies of Fenwick's reply to the editor and of his letter of pained expostulation to Lewis are not preserved in the correspondence, but the editor withdrew the paragraph in this particularly wounding form and Lewis, though not until three months had elapsed, tendered a hearty and apparently sincere apology.

Too much however must not be made of these embarrassments. Between 1872 and 1879 John Fenwick received at Thirlestaine House or corresponded with numerous scholars. In the latter year his son Thomas FitzRoy, recently down from Oxford, began to assume a share of the burden, and by 1881 most of the correspondence was answered by the son, who seems to have taken full charge of the library two years later. The young man's reception of foreign *literati* was aided by helpful letters of introduction from officials at the Bodleian and the British Museum.

Professor Mommsen who is here in London tells me that he is to go down to Cheltenham [wrote Edward Maunde Thompson from the British Museum on 29 August 1885]. I shall be very much obliged to you if you will do everything you can for him. You will find him a very pleasant man—and he speaks English very well. He is one of the most tremendous swells that they have in Germany—and at his name every German student shakes in his thick boots and knocks his shock head on the pavement in adoration. I believe he has never been known to make a mistake in his life, and he has the power of dictating ten books at a time to as many scribes. But as you are an Englishman you need not tremble—only be kind to him.

The bequest by Sir Thomas Phillipps of an immense library with wholly inadequate funds for its upkeep was out of step with the spirit of the age and invited an attempt by private Act of Parliament to free the Trustees and life-tenants from an almost insupportable burden. In the event however no such private Act was required. Even at Phillipps's death salutary legal reforms were in preparation, which culminated in the Settled Land Acts of 1882 and 1884. Under these Acts the Court of Chancery was authorized to allow the sale by trustees of chattels settled as heirlooms, however strictly the testator or settlor might have prescribed preservation by his family. The Court normally acted upon evidence by affidavit, and special relevance was attached to the wishes and financial position of the life-tenant and to the value, interest and tendency to deteriorate of the heirlooms concerned.

The life-tenants of Thirlestaine House lost no time in laying their case before the Court, and seven affidavits were submitted in November 1885, which may be studied in the Chancery Division section of the Public Record Office. The most interesting for our purpose are two sworn by Mrs Fenwick on November the third and the sixteenth. The terms of Phillipps's will were set out and it was noted that no power of sale had been given by the testator to his Trustees. It was pointed out that the manuscripts were, from the point of view of use, particularly inconveniently housed at Thirlestaine. The library was said to encumber the house and render it almost uninhabitable, and stress was laid on the fact that the contents of the mansion were not insured, and that there was no possibility of paying insurance premiums out of the available income. The house, it was pointed out, contained upwards of sixty rooms, one of them seventy feet long; and this figure did not include the kitchen block which comprised a further twenty-six rooms. Out of an income of about £1000 a year annuities had to be paid to two of the Trustees, library servants employed and charges for rates, taxes, outside repairs and heating met, leaving, as was stated above, only about £225 a year for Mrs Fenwick herself. This sum was quite insufficient to carry out internal repairs, to keep up the gardens, and to provide proper curtains, carpets and furniture which were woefully deficient. Leave was sought to sell the manuscripts, those printed books of which duplicate copies or other editions were present in the library, and the duplicate prints and coins. This, the second affidavit concluded, would still leave 'a very large collection of pictures and printed books estimated at between 60,000 and 100,000 volumes for the proper display of which more room is required'.

Mr Justice Pearson can have had few grounds for questioning the reasonableness of this application. In a judgement delivered in Chambers on 23 November 1885 he appointed, in the place of Coxwell Rogers and Gael, one new Trustee, John Richard Burton, to serve with John Haydon Cardew and he ordered 'that the Applicant be at liberty to sell (such sale to be made with the approbation of the Judge) all or any of the Manuscripts and all or any of the books of which there are duplicates or two or more editions and all or any of the prints and coins of which there are duplicates'. The way was now open for a series of dispersals which was to awaken the liveliest interest and competition in the world of books for more than sixty years.

CHAPTER III

1886-1914

Sales to governments and institutions — the Meerman group sold to the German Government — the Dutch transaction — the Belgian Government's purchases — sale of Welsh MSS. to Cardiff Public Library — the long-drawn French negotiation — the strange history of Sir Max Waechter, the Kaiser and University College, London — the British Museum combines with the Universities of Oxford and Cambridge to negotiate with Fenwick — the project fails.

Thomas FitzRoy Fenwick lost little time in preparing parts of the collection for sale. In the summer of 1886 he consigned a number of duplicate printed books to Messrs Sotheby's auction-rooms, but decided that at first he would not expose the manuscripts to similar hazards, and would instead attempt to sell them in blocks by private treaty. To this end he reprinted an expanded version of Phillipps's catalogue description of the six hundred and twenty-three Meerman manuscripts,[1] which he planned to send to libraries likely to contemplate so extensive a purchase. In the event he could have saved the expense of a printed catalogue, for his first tentative overtures met with an eager response. On 29 July 1886 Fenwick addressed himself to Theodor Mommsen.

You will probably have seen [he wrote] from notices in some of the papers that a portion of our printed books are to be sold on Aug. 3 and seven following days. We are also thinking of parting with a few of our MSS. viz. the Meerman collection....I recollect that when you were here last year you particularly requested to be informed if ever there was any chance of these MSS. being sold, as you thought that your Government would be glad of an opportunity of purchasing them *en bloc*.

Fenwick asked Mommsen to bring the matter to the notice of the head of the Royal Library at Berlin, and laid particular stress

---

[1] *Bibliotheca Phillippica: a Catalogue of the Phillipps Manuscripts, numbers 1388 to 2010* (Cheltenham, 1886).

on the desirability of keeping the transaction confidential. On 8 August Dr August Wilmanns, the Royal Librarian, expressed his keen interest in Fenwick's proposal and asked him to name a price for the entire Meerman collection: on 12 August Fenwick replied with the figure of fourteen thousand pounds.

With regard to the price mentioned [wrote Wilmanns on 21 August] I confess that I find it rather high. I am far from underrating this precious collection, but I cannot but duly observe, that among many important numbers there are also a great deal of more modern and less interesting pieces. Considering that the whole Meerman collection, nearly two-thirds of which are now in your possession, in 1824 was sold for nearly 32000 florins, I think the tenfold amount of 10000£ would be no bad offer and 12000£ a very good one.

I was somewhat surprised to find that you considered the price mentioned for the Phillipps MSS. 1388–2010 rather high [replied Fenwick on 14 September] though I was quite prepared for your remark that some of the MSS. are of inferior importance. Having myself examined each MS. I quite admit that this is so, but I would point out that if they were all of equal importance with the best MSS. of the collection £40,000 would not buy them.

You will pardon me and correct me if I am wrong, if I mention that you seem to have made a miscalculation with regard to the price of the MSS.

You say that in 1824 the Meerman collection was sold for 32000 florins & that the portion now offered for sale represents about two thirds of that price, also that you consider ten times the amount would be a fair offer.

I should certainly be very glad to accept such an offer which would represent nearly £20,000 for the two thirds.

You will therefore see from this that in asking £14,000 I am not asking anything like ten times the amount for which they were sold in 1824. I gather from your letter that in fixing a price you are chiefly guided by the sum realised at the Meerman sale.

I myself am quite convinced that the prices realised at that sale afford no criterion of the *real* value of these MSS. even at that date. If you will carefully study the prices paid for these MSS. and compare them with the prices realised for MSS. of the same class at other sales of that period you will I think come to the same conclusion.

The sale as you know took place in a country containing a very small percentage of bookbuyers, as is evidenced by the fact that so few of the MSS. were purchased by Dutch booksellers; moreover the country was at that time not too accessible for foreign purchasers, who were of course unwilling to purchase without an opportunity of inspecting the MSS.

The chief purchasers were the English booksellers, who made a very good business out of the sale by importing their purchases & selling them at considerably advanced prices.

I have no doubt you imagine that Sir Thos. Phillipps bought all his MSS. *at the sale*, but that is not the case. He purchased a large quantity of them from the booksellers & at high prices.

Again to show you that the prices realised in 1824 were in no sense fair ones I will tell you what is probably unknown to you that M. Meerman—who you will admit was a good judge of the value of MSS.—gave, in the year 1764, 120,000 francs for the 850 Clermont MSS. alone, the greater part of which are among those now offered to you.

And again as another example, take the first MS (No. 1388) in the Phillipps Catalogue 'Quatuor Evangelia *Syriace* sec XIII' (by the way this MS is wrongly dated, it should be Sec. VII) & you will find that it was sold for 125 florins, an absolutely ridiculous price even in 1824, but it was afterwards bought by Sir Thos. Phillipps who knew the true value of MSS., for very nearly ten times that amount, & so it was with most of the other MSS., as I could prove to you.

From what I have said you will see that the sum asked is *extremely small* & I think when compared with the prices paid of late years for collections of MSS. you will find that it is *quite* the most reasonable offer that has ever been made to you.

This eloquent justification left Wilmanns unconvinced, and in his reply he suggested that he should recommend the purchase to the Prussian Minister of Public Instruction for the sum of twelve thousand pounds. In a further letter of 30 October Fenwick declined to accept the lower figure. He was not acting for himself alone he explained; the money would go into trust funds and it was necessary for him to satisfy the Court of Chancery that in each transaction he had acted in the best interests of the estate. 'I think if you consider the matter a little longer', he wrote, 'you will quite understand how impossible it is to state a lower price for MSS. 1388–2010 (excluding a copy of Statius [No. 1798][1] and the Description des douze Césars [No. 1940][2] which we intend under any circumstances to retain here).' He went on to enumerate a few of the most remarkable pieces in the collection, the seventh-century Syriac Gospels [No. 1388], the tenth-century Greek Apsyrtus [No. 1538] over which Sir Frederic Madden had rhapsodized in 1844,[3] the famous *Codex Theodosianus* [No. 1761] and the *Collectio Conciliorum Galliae* [No. 1743] of the seventh and eighth centuries respectively.

On 18 November 1886 Wilmanns wrote to ask for a formal document which he could lay before the Minister, urging at the same time that the offer might be kept open until April 1887. Fenwick jibbed at this long delay, caused, Wilmanns subsequently explained, by the fact that the Prussian fiscal year began on 1 April: and the latest date which the vendor would concede was 20 January 1887. The period however had to be extended at Wilmanns's urgent request and on 10 February he wrote to ask whether Fenwick would be prepared to sell the Latin manuscripts alone from the collection, a question which met with a firm refusal. On 10 March Fenwick wrote with some asperity from St Moritz asking for a decision and a brisk exchange of telegrams followed. On 1 April Wilmanns sadly reported that the Government was unwilling to vote the whole purchase price. Might he, he asked, come to Cheltenham and pick out those manuscripts which were of particular relevance to German history? The librarian joined Fenwick at St Moritz and, as a result of their discussions, in the following month two German scholars, one of them the well-known palaeographer Wilhelm Studemund (1843–99), presented themselves at Thirlestaine House and drew up a report on the whole collection; they so strongly urged the acquisi-

---

[1] Now in Sir Chester Beatty's Library, Dublin.

[2] Sold at Sotheby's, 1 July 1946, lot 28 A; in 1954 in the hands of Libreria Antiquaria Hoepli, Milan.

[3] In his journal of 2 October 1844, Madden describes this as a noble volume 'for the beauty of the small gold capital letters quite unrivalled. It would be an ornament to any library in the world.'

tion of the entire block of Meerman manuscripts that Treasury scruples in Berlin were overcome, and on 24 June 1887 Fenwick received a telegram which stated 'The money is ready'. The Court of Chancery set its approval on the transaction a week later, and on 4 August Wilmanns reported that the crates containing many of the greatest treasures in the Phillipps Library had been safely received at Berlin.

Allowing for an error in numeration and the two items which Fenwick retained, six hundred and twenty-one manuscripts changed hands in this transaction, and according to a calculation made by Fenwick they had cost Phillipps £1503. 17s. 3d. in 1824. If this figure is correct the tenfold increase in price mentioned by Wilmanns is a good deal nearer the truth than Fenwick's strong disclaimer of 14 September 1886 would suggest. Even so, at an average price of about £22. 10s. 0d. the Meerman group must not be considered expensive at £14,000: taken all in all they were of outstanding quality, and their value today would certainly have to be computed in terms of six figures.

Messrs Sotheby's announcement of a sale by auction of material from the Phillipps Library in August 1886 brought one immediate and unsolicited inquiry to Thirlestaine House from Dr Samuel Muller, head of the Royal Archives at Utrecht. Son of Frederik Muller (1817–81), a well-known antiquarian bookseller of Amsterdam, the archivist must be commended for the enterprise and energy with which he sought to reassemble the scattered documents relating to his province. For Phillipps owned a very substantial number of Dutch manuscripts, including a great many deeds, the majority bought at Leyden in 1826 at the sale of the collection of Petrus van Musschenbroek, whose library contained many documents 'borrowed' from Dutch Record Offices by an earlier collector, Pieter Bondam.[1] Muller in a letter of 13 July 1886 expressed alarm lest this manuscript material relating to Holland should be thrown suddenly on the market at too short notice for him to make any financial arrangements for its purchase.

[1] See *Phillipps Studies*, no. 3, p. 28.

Would Fenwick therefore be disposed, he asked, to negotiate with the Netherlands Government on the subject and allow him to examine the manuscripts at Cheltenham for this purpose? On 29 July Fenwick replied that he would probably be selling the Dutch manuscripts and that he would certainly wish them to be restored intact to Holland if the matter could be arranged. In the middle of September Muller, accompanied by a young archivist named Louis van Hasselt, was cordially received at Cheltenham. It was planned that van Hasselt should draw up a report which would be submitted to the Minister of the Interior, but circumstances contrived to delay the matter. On 2 January 1887 Fenwick wrote to say that unless some move were made by the end of the month he would feel free to offer the manuscripts to another purchaser. In an apologetic reply Muller disclosed that van Hasselt, distracted both by a change of post and by impending matrimony, had not in fact put pen to paper in the matter of the report, but that he himself had now recovered van Hasselt's notes and was drawing up a memorandum. In reply to a subsequent request to make a formal proposal to the Minister Fenwick wrote on 3 March 1887 offering one hundred and seventy-six manuscripts or groups of manuscripts bearing Phillipps numbers and fourteen boxes of unnumbered deeds for the sum of £2750. At this stage negotiations on the purchaser's side were taken over by the Graaf van Bylandt, Netherlands Minister in London, upon whom Fenwick was invited to call. The Minister explained that his Government considered the price too high, and in justification of this handed him a translation of a long memorandum on the subject written by Muller. The archivist was by no means anxious to depreciate the value of the collection, nor did he think that Fenwick's price was exorbitant: nevertheless after the most careful consideration, and after receiving independent calculations from van Hasselt and from Dr Tiele, Librarian of Utrecht University, he could really not in conscience recommend his Government to pay more than £2000 for the collection. On 3 September 1887 Fenwick wrote a twelve-page reply to van Bylandt, answering Muller's memorandum point by point. He sent a copy to Muller, and on 17 September he politely declined the latter's suggestion that the deadlock might be broken by resorting to arbitration by some neutral authority of universally acknowledged distinction and integrity, such as Léopold Delisle, of the Bibliothèque Nationale, or Wilhelm Wattenbach, editor of the *Monumenta Germaniae Historica*. On 15 November the Netherlands Minister communicated to Fenwick his Government's decision to abide by the figure of £2000 as its maximum offer, producing in support an even longer report from Muller in which he politely but firmly controverted Fenwick's arguments for a higher sum. We have no way of knowing whether Fenwick was moved by the cogency of his reasoning or crushed by the sheer weight of correspondence and memoranda, but he agreed to accept the lower figure, a wise decision since if many of the Dutch manuscripts were not sold to the Netherlands Government it was difficult to envisage any other purchaser for them. The Court of Chancery approved the sale on 6 December 1887 but a long argument about legal expenses and the mode of payment delayed the signing of a contract until 2 February 1888, and a further month intervened before Muller visited Cheltenham and triumphantly carried off the manuscripts for which he had opened negotiations eighteen months before. Praise is due to him for the courtesy, tact and pertinacity with which he conducted his campaign not only against an obdurate vendor but also against a legalistic officialdom in his own country which came near to thwarting his designs.[1]

An application from the Belgian Government was received by Fenwick while the Dutch negotiation was in progress. It would appear that in April 1887 Fenwick had some conversation on the subject of a possible sale with Charles Ruelens, keeper of manuscripts at the Bibliothèque Royale, Brussels, as a result of which the head of the library, Edouard Fétis (1812–1909), wrote an exploratory letter on 1 June. He had, he said, received authority

---

[1] This account of the purchase of MSS. by the Netherlands Government is abridged from a much fuller version which appeared in *Het Boek* (xxxiii, i).

from the Minister of Agriculture, under whose jurisdiction Letters, Sciences and Arts lay, to treat with Fenwick, and delegates had been nominated who would inspect any Belgian manuscript material available. At the outset, however, he required reassurance on two points. The first had been raised by the Minister himself. Rumour reported that the heirs of Sir Thomas Phillipps set so high a price on his manuscripts that there was little chance of coming to terms with them. While it was true that Fenwick's previous conversation with M. Ruelens had not given this impression, the Minister would welcome a few lines on the precise manner in which it was intended that the negotiations should be conducted. Secondly Fétis requested that the usual charges for consulting manuscripts at Thirlestaine House should be waived in the case of the inspecting representatives of Belgium.

In a reply of 4 June Fenwick dismissed the charge of exorbitant prices as 'utterly without foundation', and stated that of course no charge would be made to scholars who were inspecting manuscripts with a view to their purchase. He went on to explain that the Court of Chancery had to set its approval on any transaction, and laid down three preliminary conditions in his turn. In the first place the negotiations were to be strictly private; secondly he should be supplied in advance with the names and professions of the Belgian delegates; and thirdly any notes taken in the course of their examination should be used only for the purpose of their valuation, and in particular nothing should be published without Fenwick's consent in writing. On 29 June Fétis accepted these terms without demur. The Belgian delegates were disclosed as Charles Piot (1812–99), Archivist-General, and Charles Ruelens. The Minister had also attached to the mission the veteran historian and politician Baron Kervyn de Lettenhove, explaining however that he would not be available when the important question of purchase came up for debate in the Legislative Chambers.

After several postponements all three delegates visited Cheltenham during September. Unfortunately Ruelens, for whom Fenwick quickly developed a warm regard, was taken ill on his return to Brussels, and the final agreement had to be postponed until April 1888, when Fenwick contracted to sell two hundred and eleven manuscripts, a large proportion of them medieval books on vellum from Belgian religious houses, for the sum of £1652. 11s. 0d. Encouraged by this successful conclusion, reached without serious disagreement, Ruelens visited Thirlestaine House again in June, armed with authority to proceed further. On this occasion he agreed to buy for £585. 10s. one hundred and six manuscripts which had once formed part of the medieval library of the Cistercian abbey of Aulne-sur-Sambre. To Baron Solvyns, the Belgian Minister in London, fell the task of arranging for the collection of the manuscripts and for payment, the latter as usual involving legal complications, caused in the main by the fact that Fenwick's mother was the true life-tenant of the library and not Fenwick himself. On 31 August however Ruelens wrote happily from Brussels saying that the Prime Minister had inspected with enthusiasm the newly unpacked accessions to the Royal Library and had complimented Ruelens and Piot on the success of their operations.

A further transaction with the Royal Library took place between September and December 1890. Ruelens unhappily was too sick a man to travel to England, but he sent a list of manuscripts for which he offered £400. Some of these were no longer available and Fenwick countered with his own list. Some friendly bargaining ended in a compromise, and on 8 December Fétis wrote accepting Fenwick's proposal, explaining that Ruelens was once again absent from his desk owing to illness. Five days later Fenwick received news of his death. 'I cannot tell you', he wrote to Fétis on 29 December, 'how deeply grieved I was to hear of the sad termination of M. Ruelens's illness. It was indeed a great shock to me...and I deeply regret that he did not live to see the success-ful termination of his efforts to enrich the Royal Library....I shall never forget the friendly and kindly spirit in which he acted towards me in carrying out the former negotiations & I had always hoped to see him here on another visit.'

The goodwill towards the Royal Library which Ruelens had established extended to his successor as Keeper of Manuscripts, R.P. J. Van den Gheyn, who in the winter of 1899 was able to buy a further hundred and seventy manuscripts, some of considerable importance, a vast mass of charters relating to Tournai, and two hundred and thirty-nine volumes of catalogues of Belgian and Dutch libraries for the sum of £2570. Between 1887 and 1900 the Belgian Government spent £5208 on the purchase by private treaty of Phillipps manuscripts, and spent it to excellent advantage. For a figure which half a dozen of the early items alone would command today, Belgium acquired nearly six hundred manuscripts and a very large number of deeds, a token restitution for the terrible depredations which Belgian libraries suffered in the early years of the nineteenth century.

There is a wearisome similarity about these transactions which prompts me to relegate three of comparatively minor importance to a footnote.[1] Mention must be made however of a commendable demonstration of Welsh patriotism whereby Cardiff Public Library acquired in 1896 a large block of manuscripts relating to the Principality. In March 1895 the Library Committee authorized its representatives to treat with Fenwick, who collected together his Welsh material for inspection by Professor Thomas Powel and the Cardiff Librarian. The price asked was £3491. 15s. 0d. together with a commission of 5 per cent to Messrs Sotheran and Co., who acted for the purchasers. This was a substantial sum to be found by a Library Committee whose annual allocation available for the purchase of books was only at that time about £650. Nevertheless Powel and the Librarian urged the importance of preserving the Welsh manuscripts from dispersal in terms which

---

[1] Between 1889 and 1894 negotiations took place which led to the sale of a collection of documents relating to Bordeaux for £800; the manuscripts were secured by the Archives du Département de la Gironde through the agency of M. Brutails, the archivist. In 1890 and 1891 a similar sale of deeds and manuscripts took place to two record offices in Alsace-Lorraine. The sum involved was £685 and the negotiator Dr Wolfram. In 1904 Fenwick was persuaded by Professor Ignazio Giorgi to sell a single manuscript (No. 12335) to the Biblioteca Casanatense, Rome.

spurred the Committee to seek help in their bold design. John Cory, a liberal friend of the Library, not only offered £500 himself, but undertook with five or six others, several of them members of the Library Committee, to become guarantors to the bank of the overdraft for the whole price. The purchase was completed, and several private subscribers came forward, notably Lord Bute who gave £1000: in this way over half the total figure was raised. The balance was paid in instalments from Library funds over the succeeding ten years. Cardiff secured about seven hundred manuscripts or groups of manuscripts bearing Phillipps numbers, including the famous text of Aneirin's *Gododdin* (16614), an accession which made its Public Library an important centre for Welsh historical studies. Committees do not always rise to the occasion and seize fleeting opportunities, and those gentlemen of Cardiff, in whose hands lay the administration of the Library in 1896, merit the gratitude of all Welsh scholars.

I must chronicle at some length a marathon negotiation transacted with great patience and skill on behalf of the French Government between 1904 and 1908 by Henri Omont (1857–1940), Keeper of Manuscripts at the Bibliothèque Nationale. Over one hundred and ten letters were exchanged and their reader is left with an agreeable impression of Omont's tact, pertinacity and imperturbability in the face of numerous set-backs. On 24 January 1904 he sent Fenwick offprints from *Bibliothèque de l'École des Chartes*[1] and from *Revue des Bibliothèques* describing Phillipps manuscripts which had been bought by the Bibliothèque Nationale at Sotheby's auction in the previous year. It was much to be hoped, he said, that the national library would continue gradually to reassemble the vast collection of manuscripts relating to France, which were housed at Cheltenham. There were indeed financial

[1] LXIV (1903), pp. 490–553. Omont wrote a number of articles describing manuscripts in the Phillipps Collection: 'Manuscrits relatifs à l'histoire de France conservés dans la bibliothèque de Sir Thomas Phillipps à Cheltenham' (*Bibliothèque de l'École des Chartes*, L (1889), pp. 68–96 and 180–217); 'Manuscrits relatifs à L'Histoire de Paris et l'Île-de-France conservés à Cheltenham' (*Bulletin de la Société de l'Histoire de Paris et de l'Île-de-France*, XVI (1889), pp. 43–53).

difficulties but these might perhaps be overcome in a variety of ways. For example might not Fenwick be disposed to sell a block of material to the Bibliothèque Nationale regularly every year, or at least to give Omont long notice of the appearance of French material in the auction-room so that proper financial provision could be made well in advance? There was yet another scheme which might be worth exploring. Would Fenwick consider selling a large block of manuscripts at one time and allowing payment to be made by regular annual instalments?

On 6 February Fenwick replied cordially. He would, he said, welcome an opportunity to sell the whole of the French collections to the Bibliothèque Nationale. Could not Omont borrow the money for this transaction and repay, not Fenwick, but the lender by a regular allocation from his annual budget? In the following May Omont proposed a visit to Cheltenham in the company of Paul Meyer for the purpose of discussing the prospects of a bulk purchase. He sent Fenwick a list of two hundred and fifty manuscripts which they wished to inspect and asked the vendor if he would set an individual value on each one. This however Fenwick refused to do.

Omont's visit was duly made at the end of May, but it was not until 12 October that he made his proposal. A selection of Phillipps's manuscripts, he suggested, should be reserved for the Bibliothèque Nationale, which would guarantee to buy them at the rate of one thousand pounds' worth annually. Fenwick, however, declined this instalment plan and asked for other proposals. Several letters were exchanged in which Omont expatiated on the annual budgetary system as it affected French institutions, while Fenwick countered with his view that the Court of Chancery was unlikely to accept any form of payment other than a lump sum. On 9 November Fenwick at last sent Omont a list of manuscripts which he valued at £4510, to which Omont replied on 25 November that since his valuation of the same list amounted to only £2615 he presumed that any hope of a successful conclusion must be abandoned. On 26 December, however, he wrote again. He had, he said, sought fresh advice, this time from a historian who was disposed to take a more generous view of the value of the manuscripts than a librarian: and in consequence he was able to raise the Bibliothèque Nationale's offer to £3619: and Fenwick, not to be outdone in concession, reduced his figure to £3735. At last it looked as though the gap could be bridged, but unhappily at this point Léopold Delisle, head of the Bibliothèque Nationale, retired, and on 21 February 1905 Omont announced that the matter must be suspended until his successor was appointed.

During the pause a fresh scrutiny of Fenwick's and Omont's lists of manuscripts revealed the fact that they were not identical, and that several manuscripts which Omont particularly desired had been omitted from the block offered by Fenwick at £3735: and when Fenwick declined to amend his list the negotiations were again suspended by Omont on 1 June 1905. In an attempt to break the deadlock Fenwick added some, but not all, of the contested manuscripts and put the price up to £4000: but, since Omont's efforts to raise funds from the Minister of Public Instruction had been based on a list which contained all the items under dispute, he did not feel able to proceed. On 28 June 1905 he wrote congratulating Fenwick on his marriage, and explaining that constitutionally the Bibliothèque Nationale was unlike the British Museum in so far as the Minister was much more intimately concerned with its affairs, and had personally to approve large transactions and to include them in his annual budget. On 8 October 1905 Omont suggested that an attempt might be made to get the money voted for 1906, but there was still the discrepancy in the list to be got over. On 12 October Fenwick sent a fresh list, valued at £4120, but Omont was adamant that his original schedule must be the basis for any transaction. At this stage the inclusion of only an additional five manuscripts was the point at issue, and in a real effort to reach an agreement Fenwick added three of them, raising his price by only ten pounds. Omont however insisted that the Minister had stipulated that all five manuscripts must be ceded and refused to relinquish his claim to the final two.[1] This time Fenwick broke off negotiations in a friendly letter of 18 November 1905.

I greatly regret [he wrote] as you do, that our efforts have had no result, & that your Minister was not prepared to make any concessions in response to my endeavours to arrive at an understanding. I particularly regret that the negotiations with your country have failed.... Let me again thank you for all the trouble you have taken, & remind you that if, in the future, you should at any time wish for extracts from, or particulars of any of our MSS. you have, as in the past, only to write to me.

At this point Delisle produced a plan which would have circumvented the French Minister's refusal to conclude a bargain without the two manuscripts. He would propose, he suggested, that the whole collection should be acquired by the Musée Condé at Chantilly and that the Institut Français should be asked to vote the purchase price. He stipulated, however, that one of the two disputed books should be ceded, and in this matter Fenwick was firm in his refusal. Delisle therefore did not bring his plan before the Institut. This was in November 1905 and I may perhaps be forgiven if I omit an account of the next two years' negotiations, which 'ces deux maudits manuscrits' continued to bedevil. In November 1907 a serious attempt was made to begin afresh. Omont suggested that a new list should be constructed, one which would omit the two bones of contention. He submitted it to Fenwick, who on 17 December valued its contents at £4050. In fact, however, it emerged that Omont's 'new' list was one which Fenwick had already priced two years before at £80 less: but when Omont questioned his figure Fenwick asserted that he had prepared an entirely new valuation without any reference to the former list and that the total of £4050 must stand. On 10 February 1908 Omont wrote his acceptance, suggesting at the same time

[1] They were Nos. 4760, 'Registrum Epistolarum Papae Innocentii 6ti, fol. v. s. xiv', and 10190, 'Ansegisi Capitularia Regum Francorum, Obl. 4to. v. s. ix.' The former is in the possession of Messrs Lionel and Philip Robinson and the latter in Sir Chester Beatty's Library, Dublin.

a visit to Cheltenham in March to collect the manuscripts. Before the visit several letters were exchanged on the subject of a supplementary purchase but Fenwick was emphatic in his refusal to begin a second negotiation before the first had been safely concluded. On Omont's arrival however he relented to the extent of selling a further small group for £75, making £4125 in all. Three benefactors, Barons James and Edmond de Rothschild and Maurice Fenaille, made substantial contributions towards the purchase price, and on 2 May 1908 Omont announced to Fenwick the safe arrival of one of the most important accessions of manuscripts ever received by the Bibliothèque Nationale. The collection comprised two hundred and seventy-two manuscripts, among them thirty cartularies dating from the eleventh century, two early collections of the Statutes of the University of Paris, the first register of the Parliament of Poictiers, and a very large collection of charters from the tenth century onwards. Omont described the whole group in a special catalogue published the following year.[1]

The transactions so far described, though many of them have been protracted and characterized by hard bargaining, have been reasonably straightforward. It remains to describe a further negotiation in two phases, one of which presents several mysterious features and poses problems which have remained partially insoluble.

On 6 March 1909 Fenwick was approached by Professor Robert Priebsch of University College, London, who knew the German manuscripts in the Phillipps collection well, having described many of them in print.[2] Priebsch was an Austrian; he had previously held a post at Liverpool, and his appointment to a London chair had done much to raise the standard of German

---

[1] *Catalogue des manuscrits latins et français de la collection Phillipps acquis en 1908 pour la Bibliothèque Nationale* (Paris, 1908). Omont added a useful finding-list of Phillipps manuscripts which he had traced in other libraries.

[2] *Deutsche Handschriften in England*, I (1896), pp. 42–142: for other accounts of Phillipps MSS. relating to Germany see the series of articles by G. H. Pertz in *Archiv*, VII (1839), pp. 95–101 and IX (1847), pp. 498–500; also R. Pauli, *Neues Archiv*, II (1877), pp. 429–32; G. Waitz, *ibid.* IV (1879), pp. 585–608; F. Liebermann, *ibid.* X (1884), pp. 588–94; K. Hampe, *ibid.* XXII (1897), pp. 673–93.

studies in that University. He had in particular built up an excellent German departmental library at University College, with the co-operation of R. W. Chambers, at that time College Librarian. Priebsch explained to Fenwick that it was his particular desire to secure a group of medieval German manuscripts as research material. Would Fenwick, he asked, consider the sale of such a group if Priebsch could find a benefactor who would foot the bill? On 10 March Fenwick replied sympathetically and suggested that he should call on Priebsch on some occasion when he was in London. The two men met in May and Priebsch handed over a list of about a hundred manuscripts which he was anxious to buy. Fenwick seems to have been dilatory about setting a price on them, but in September 1910 Priebsch wrote that he had a particular benefactor in mind and that it was therefore necessary for Fenwick to arrive at a figure. Another meeting took place and it would appear that the sum of £3000 was named, but Fenwick heard nothing more until he received a letter dated 24 February 1911, asking whether R. W. Chambers and Priebsch might look again at the manuscripts and draw up a detailed report on them.

Unhappily Fenwick, thinking that Priebsch's benefactor was unlikely to materialize, had consigned some of the manuscripts to Sotheby's and on 25 February he sent a telegram to Priebsch which stated, 'Very unfortunate considerable part of collection catalogued for sale in April'. Priebsch, who had assumed that before taking any step of this nature Fenwick would have informed him, was naturally disappointed. He had, he told Fenwick, set his heart on acquiring the collection and had worked hard to find a purchaser. He assumed however that his option on the purchase of the collection still held good provided that he could find a purchaser before the sale-catalogue appeared. In a polite letter of 27 February Fenwick replied that the auction must take place as planned. It was two years, he pointed out, since Priebsch had said that he would find a purchaser, and in any case he denied that University College had ever had a firm option on the group of German manuscripts at £3000, certainly not for an indefinite period. And so the matter remained, despite a further appeal by Priebsch in person. All however was not lost, for a fund was quickly opened to which a number of friends of University College, especially Lord Crawford, made donations. The sum of £408 was raised, and at the Phillipps sale at Sotheby's on 24 April 1911 Priebsch contrived to buy fifteen medieval German manuscripts for the College.

If Priebsch's first attempt to buy Phillipps manuscripts ended unsatisfactorily, his second can only be described as disastrous, though no blame can be attached either to himself or to Fenwick. On 8 February 1912 the Professor wrote once more to Fenwick, asking whether he and the Secretary of University College, Walter Seton, might call upon him. Fenwick was in London and therefore able to arrange a meeting on the following day, when the two representatives of University College explained that an opportunity had arisen of receiving another benefaction for the purchase of German manuscripts. Fenwick duly prepared a second list of manuscripts, which were inspected at Cheltenham in the middle of March by Priebsch and Seton. They secured an option expiring on 15 April 1912 to buy the collection for £2500. On 25 March Seton telegraphed an offer of £2000, but this was declined.

On 9 April he wrote as follows:

I am glad to be now in a position to tell you that we are now able to close with your offer to sell for Two Thousand Five Hundred Pounds the collection of German manuscripts about which you have been in correspondence with Professor Priebsch and myself and which you showed to us on our visit to Cheltenham on March 20th.

The negotiations in this matter have been difficult and delicate and until today I have not been in a position to send a formal acceptance of the offer. My next point is a confidential one. For important reasons with which I need not trouble you, the collection will be bought not in the name of the College, but of the intending donor who is Sir Max Waechter of Richmond. The fact is at present known only to the principals in the negotiations and Sir Max Waechter particularly wishes that his name should not be disclosed, except of course if and when necessary to the Court of Chancery. Sir Max would accordingly be glad if you would now be good enough to take steps as soon as possible to secure the necessary authority from the Court of Chancery for the sale. There are again reasons why it is desirable that this order should be obtained with as little delay as possible and I should be glad if you could in replying give me some idea of the number of days the application is likely to take, judging by previous experience.

Fenwick answered by return of post, expressing his particular gratification that the manuscripts were to remain in England. He would of course respect the purchaser's wish that his name should not be made public, and had already written to his solicitors about an application to the Court. 'The Donor is pressing very hard to know when he can complete', replied Seton on 13 April, suggesting that he might be able to get some influence brought to bear upon Sir John Macdonell, one of the Masters in Chancery, whereby the matter could be hurried forward. Five days later the Court formalities were completed and on 20 April Seton himself collected the manuscripts from Cheltenham, signing on behalf of Sir Max Waechter a detailed receipt headed 'List of MSS. according to Phillipps Cat. of MSS. sold to Sir Max Waechter with a view to being given to University College London'.

'It was with the greatest astonishment and annoyance', wrote Fenwick six years later, 'that when visiting the Royal Library in Berlin in May 1914 I heard from one of the officials that the MSS., which I imagined safely housed in University College, had been presented by Sir Max Waechter to the Royal Library.' The chain of events which led to this unexpected termination can be partially reconstructed, though there are several gaps in the story.

Sir Max Leonard Waechter (1837–1924) was born at Stettin. He settled early in England and became naturalized in 1865. He was a lifelong Liberal, High Sheriff of Surrey in 1902, and was active in many philanthropic projects, in particular the founding of homes for convalescents and old people. Like many other Anglo-Germans he viewed with grave concern the deterioration of relations between Great Britain and Germany, as an antidote to which he founded the European Unity League. When the negotiations for the purchase of Fenwick's German manuscripts had been almost completed he hit upon a plan which seemed to him to offer an opportunity of a gesture of *rapprochement* between the two countries. Instead of giving the manuscripts direct to University College he offered them as a present to the German Emperor, on the understanding that the Kaiser personally would give half to University College and half to the Royal Library at Berlin. In reply to this offer Waechter received, in his own words, 'a letter from some high official in Germany pointing out that it would be impossible for the Emperor to accept a gift with conditions attached. I looked upon this as a mere question of etiquette and withdrew my conditions.' The purchase was then completed. It will be observed that Priebsch was not associated with the final phase of the transaction. The burden of carrying it through fell upon Seton alone, and while he cannot be acquitted of some degree of duplicity towards Fenwick in the matter, one can sympathize with him as the victim of circumstances which lay largely outside his control. After remaining for a period at University College the manuscripts were forwarded to Germany, Waechter firmly believing that a gentleman's agreement had been concluded whereby half of them would find their home in London; and the head of the Royal Library, Adolf von Harnack, well known as a theologian, assumed responsibility for the division with University College. It may be, of course, that he was not fully apprised of the circumstances of the gift, though Waechter afterwards asserted that the whole correspondence had been forwarded to him. At all events no single manuscript of any importance was allocated to University College, which received ninety-nine late documents, mostly relating to the administration of Swiss towns.[1]

'My indignation at this proceeding', wrote Waechter in 1918,

---

[1] See D. K. Coveney, *Descriptive Catalogue of the Manuscripts in the Library of University College, London* (1935), Appendix II describing MSS. Phill. 1–99.

'was very great, and I placed the whole case before Prince Lichnowsky, the German Ambassador in London. He disapproved strongly of the German proceeding and promised to get it rectified, but he was evidently unsuccessful.' During the period immediately before 1914 Lichnowsky doubtless had other matters to occupy him. There is a rather tantalizing reference to the subject on the German side in the preface which Adolf von Harnack contributed to a catalogue of the manuscripts, printed in 1917 as the third volume of *Mitteilungen aus der Kgl. Bibliothek*. The writer explained that the collection, known as Sir Max Waechter's gift, owed its presence in the Royal Library to the generosity of the Kaiser, to whom Waechter had magnanimously given it for disposal at his absolute discretion. 'The interesting prelude to the gift', the preface continues, 'which was performed in London, and in which the present director of Freiburg University Library, Prof. Dr Jacobs, played an important role, cannot as yet be recounted.' It could be disclosed however, added von Harnack, that amongst the relevant correspondence was a letter from Lord Haldane to Waechter, dated 28 March 1912, in which he wrote that the gift would 'promote that feeling of the solidarity of international interests which you and I know that he [the Kaiser] has deeply at heart'.

In three of the principals in the story the episode left a permanent feeling of resentment. Fenwick felt that Seton had been less than straightforward with him, and that, while no formal condition had been attached to the sale, there had been a clear understanding that the manuscripts were being kept together in this country. Waechter felt that Adolf von Harnack had failed to honour a gentleman's agreement and that his own clearly expressed intention in making the gift had been cynically disregarded. Priebsch on the other hand laid the blame at the door of the German Emperor, whom he firmly believed to have been personally involved in the matter. Indeed he assured Dr Dorothy Coveney that the Emperor himself had promised to send a free gift of manuscripts for the library in the event of the College withdrawing from the transaction, 'and all he sent', he added, flushing purple, 'was that rubbish'.[1]

The reader may well ask why the British alone, among half the governments of Western Europe, failed to purchase a substantial block of Phillipps manuscripts direct from the Fenwick family. It was not for want of trying. Up to 1891 continuous attempts were made by both Edward Maunde Thompson, Principal Librarian of the British Museum, and by Edward Nicholson, Bodley's Librarian, to come to terms with the owners; and with these efforts, pursued at first separately and later in concert, the University of Cambridge was also associated.

On 3 August 1882 Nicholson, who had held the office of Librarian for six months, informed John Fenwick that he had been reading the painful files which dealt with the abortive negotiations with Phillipps himself. Was there now, he asked, any chance of reopening the question? In a long reply of 5 August Fenwick explained the difficulties involved, in particular the necessity of promoting an Act of Parliament to permit the sale of entailed property. On 10 August Nicholson expressed his willingness to help in the promotion of such legislation, but the passing of the Settled Land Acts did away with the need for a private bill. Six years later Nicholson was working in earnest on the project, preparing lists of manuscripts in certain select classes from Phillipps's privately printed catalogue—classical, Biblical and patristic, liturgical, antiquarian and historical, English, and Keltic (as

---

[1] I am most grateful to three correspondents for their help in unravelling this tangled story: to Dr Dorothy Coveney, who knew Priebsch well, discussed the matter with him and catalogued the manuscripts in question; to Mr Joseph W. Scott, Librarian of University College, who kindly consulted on my behalf Mr John Wilks, his predecessor in office, Dr Wilfrid Bonser and Dr Richard Offor, all three of whom were Assistant Librarians under R. W. Chambers during the first decade of the century; and to Dr Helmut Boese of the Handschriftenabteilung, Deutsche Staatsbibliothek, Berlin. Unfortunately the relevant records both of the Berlin Library and University College, London, did not survive the war. The observations made in 1918 by Fenwick and Waechter are derived from two unidentified press cuttings filed by Fenwick among his correspondence with Priebsch and Seton. It must be remembered that their remarks may have been coloured by wartime animosities.

Nicholson always wrote the word). On 8 June 1888 FitzRoy Fenwick approved in general this method of approach, while reserving at the same time his right to add or subtract from any of Nicholson's groups. Nicholson's original lists were very short, and on 27 September 1888 Fenwick made it plain that in no circumstances would he sell the plums only from the library and that Nicholson would have to enlarge the lists considerably.

As early as January 1886 Nicholson had sounded Thompson on the possibility of a joint approach, and on 11 March 1889 he wrote more specifically. The Curators of the Bodleian, he said, thought it most undesirable that libraries should raise prices against each other. Oxford might be able to spend between five and six thousand pounds on manuscripts and it would be most helpful if some concerted action could be devised. In his reply of 2 April Thompson disclosed that he had been seeking help from the Treasury. 'We came to the conclusion', he wrote, 'that for our purpose (or for that of any English Library) £20,000 ought to get us all we want.' The Treasury, after a long delay, had countered with a proposal to allow the British Museum a special grant of £2000 a year for three years. Fenwick, however, had refused to open negotiations on this basis and Thompson recommended that the matter should be allowed to rest for a while 'so as not to encourage the Fenwicks', who were apt to entertain, he asserted, 'a very exalted opinion of the value of the library'. When the time was ripe, however, Thompson agreed that he would certainly support the idea of a joint approach by the Museum and the Bodleian with about £10,000 to spend between them. On 17 June 1889 the Curators made a formal request to the Trustees of the Museum to join them in the enterprise, and set to work to raise money for the purpose. On 11 February 1890 Convocation, after a long and careful statement by Andrew Clark, the Junior Proctor, approved without opposition the allocation of £5000 from University funds. A committee of Curators was set up consisting of Clark, Max Müller, Ingram Bywater and J. L. G. Mowat, to act with the officers of the library in selecting manuscripts.

In the meantime Thompson had persuaded the Treasury to make a special grant of £10,000 to the Museum, and in reporting this to Nicholson he announced that Cambridge, too, was likely to join the party. Here the initiative appears to have come from F. W. Maitland, Downing Professor of Laws and a Syndic of the University Library, and H. R. Luard, Registrary to the University. On 3 March 1890 the Council of the Senate recommended that the Library Syndicate should have £5000 at their disposal, a sum which was to be provided from the profits of the University Press. On 6 March the Council's proposal was publicly discussed by the Senate.[1] The Librarian, Francis Jenkinson, explained the circumstances under which the University had been invited to join the British Museum and Oxford in securing those parts of the Phillipps Collection which it was desirable to keep in this country. Two speakers then asked for further information and a third, Edward Atkinson, Master of Clare since 1856, opposed the project both on financial grounds and also because Cambridge would be 'competing with two powerful bodies who would probably be better able to get for themselves the MSS. they chiefly desired'. In an eloquent speech Maitland supported the Council's recommendation. No puffing of the Middle Hill Library was necessary, he asserted; its value had long been known throughout the civilized world. Outside Oxford and Cambridge and the British Museum, there was no such collection in England. It was of such importance that the proprietors were able to charge a guinea a day for consulting the MSS. This charge had in some cases known privately to himself proved to be prohibitive. He stressed the extraordinary range of Phillipps's purchases, the inadequacy of the catalogues and the loss to scholarship which would be caused by the collection's dispersal. The nation had trusted the University Library with an enormous privilege, he said, and the nation might fairly ask something in return. He could not see what better return the University could make than that proposed; he would almost go so far as to say it would be a duty for the University to

[1] *Cambridge University Reporter*, No. 826, 11 March 1890, pp. 532–4.

do this even if it had to declare itself bankrupt the day after it was done.

Maitland's views were endorsed by Luard, who took the opportunity of expressing his sense of Fenwick's great courtesy towards himself and other scholars. He was followed by the Master of Peterhouse, James Porter, who reassured the Senate that the plan was financially sound from the point of view of the University Press. Some light relief was provided by a well-known eccentric, James Mayo of Trinity College, who habitually spoke at discussions in the Senate House, usually prefacing his remarks by the statement that he 'knew nothing of the subject in question'. On this occasion Mayo explained that he joined the opposition because he had a better plan for the disposal of the accumulated riches of the University Press. Let the Syndics make economies in the Press itself and reduce its exorbitant printing bills. There was only one comforting aspect, he added, if the University did decide to spend £5000 in this way. In that case their 'Physical Science friends could not possibly come on the University for any more money for two years at least for the promotion of Physical Ignorance'. After three more members of the Senate had spoken the Vice-Chancellor closed the discussion with a strong plea from the chair that the University would not be found inadequate in seizing this unique opportunity. At a Congregation on 13 March 1890 the Grace for providing the money duly passed the Senate.

Thompson was thus empowered to spend £20,000 on behalf of the three institutions, and he urged upon Nicholson the desirability of keeping the arrangements between the libraries strictly secret. 'The family know nothing about the real value of their collections,' he wrote on 17 December 1889, 'and consequently, while I do not believe that they would willingly overrate things, still, if they see one or other of us particularly anxious about certain mss. they may be tempted to put on fancy prices. This is only natural. Again, they may think to play us off against each other, if they should detect anything like rivalry between us.' He was also disposed to belittle 'young Fenwick's' considerable commercial acumen. 'He has no experience,' he wrote in the same letter, 'and has only picked up his market-knowledge of prices haphazard—such a man is always uncertain, and he will require careful handling, as is always the case when dealing with ignorance.' Nicholson, who had already had seven years' intermittent and fruitless dealings with Fenwick, can hardly have needed this warning, nor Thompson's further prediction that 'at any moment we may come to grief through some impracticable caprice'.

In March 1890 Thompson formally offered to spend £20,000 on behalf of the three libraries, payable over two years. Fenwick in his reply sought to set on the negotiations the term of six months, beginning in the middle of April 1890, a period unrealistically short when dealing with two academic bodies whose Long Vacations stretched from June to October. On 2 April all the interested parties conferred in London and the minute circulated afterwards shows some progress.

A meeting was held at the British Museum.

Present: Mr T. FitzRoy Fenwick
The Principal Librarian of the Museum
The Keeper of the MSS.
The Assistant-Keeper
Bodley's Librarian
The Librarian of Cambridge University.

Mr Fenwick agreed to allow till July 1891 for the purchase by the combined libraries. He stated that the romances and the illuminated MSS. were not for sale, but that if it ever was determined to sell them the combined libraries should have the first offer. By illuminated MSS. were to be understood MSS. sufficiently illuminated to be thereby enhanced in value. He also said that some sets might be kept together e.g. Cartularies, though possibly these might be separated according to Counties.

The remainder of the minute relates to the divisions in which the select manuscripts should be grouped. Eight general groups were envisaged, British topography, history, classics, literary correspondence, general literature, Bibles and liturgies, other theology and Oriental manuscripts. At Oxford the Selection Committee got to work with great energy. Already in January Nicholson had produced for the Curators printed lists of his own choice from the Phillipps Catalogue in several classes. The Committee co-opted several distinguished specialists, among them Reginald Lane Poole, John Rhys and William Sanday; and a good deal of correspondence passed between them and the Librarian. Fresh lists were drawn up, including one of Biblical and patristic manuscripts by Sanday prefaced with an interesting and able statement of the general considerations which should govern the choice of manuscripts for an institutional library.

During part of May 1890 the Keeper of Manuscripts at the British Museum, George Frederic Warner, worked at Cheltenham making his valuation of the various classes of manuscripts which Fenwick grouped together for his inspection. The division by subject was a fruitful source of disagreement, and in the field of history in particular Warner seems to have found Fenwick's selection arbitrary and unsatisfactory. On behalf of the Bodleian the Sub-Librarian, Falconer Madan, also examined several of the groups of manuscripts and made his own independent valuation. At Oxford Nicholson set a member of the staff to work extracting from old catalogues the prices which Phillipps himself had paid for the items many years before, and these figures, laboriously collected, were collated with Madan's. At Cambridge the tempo of operations was by comparison languid. Some lists were drawn up in the Library including one by Maitland of the manuscripts relating to English medieval law; but Jenkinson seems to have arranged no inspection nor attempted a valuation. Cambridge would be happy, he wrote to Nicholson on 6 June 1890, to accept the British Museum's findings and independent action would be waste of time.

On 10 June 1890 Thompson reported progress to Nicholson.

Our men examined three classes of the Phillipps MSS. [he wrote] (a) Latin Classics. 470 MSS. the greater number were late, 15th century Italian copies. Only 65 were valued at £10 and upwards, The total valuation £2,800. (b) Bibles and Service Books. This class was so mixed up with commentaries and theology, that as a class it was spoilt.

346 MSS.—221 being of the class Bibles; and 125 Service Books. Total estimate £4,700. 24 MSS. were valued at £50 and upwards. (c) Greek MSS. of all sorts 278 in all. Only 24 were priced at £10 and upwards. Total valuation £1,300. They began on History but shut up when they found they were being overpowered with all sorts.

The Latin Classics were selected as the first subject of negotiation, and Fenwick was invited to set a price upon them. On 9 July 1890 he offered them to Thompson for the sum of £7150, a figure which the latter described to Nicholson as exorbitant. Fenwick stipulated moreover that the offer must be accepted or rejected within a month, and Thompson found this condition 'very peremptory'. 'We do not at all feel inclined to accept Mr Fenwick's estimate', he wrote to Nicholson, 'and, I presume, neither will you do so. The real question is whether it is worth while for us to go on.' On 16 October Thompson disclosed a change of plan. He had talked with Fenwick, he said, and arranged that the latter should select 500 manuscripts, set a price on them and offer them to the three libraries for acceptance or refusal. 'His ideas of classes', he wrote, 'were so arbitrary that it seemed impossible to come to any arrangement with him on that line—so we might make another experiment.' A month later Fenwick offered five hundred and fifty manuscripts for the sum of £10,000, a proposal which Thompson passed to the Department of Manuscripts for comment.

I have with the help of Mr Warner [reported Edward Scott of that Department in a memorandum of 18 November] carefully gone through all the numbers in the enclosed list, and compared them with the notes and prices of the same, furnished by us in last May and June. I find that out of the 550 MSS. here selected we saw and priced 250, or very nearly half of them. Our valuation of these came to £1,565.9.0, or about £6 per head. Mr Fenwick asks for twice the number £10,000, or about £18 per head.

Scott went on to complain that Fenwick's selection contained not one first class MS., and not more than a dozen that we should be anxious to secure at a sale. Nine tenths of them we should absolutely decline to recommend the Trustees to purchase. Of the half we did *not* see, the descriptions in the Phillipps Catalogue, meagre as they are, are yet sufficient to show us that the MSS. themselves are, if possible, inferior to the half we did see. Not a single classic, nor chartulary, nor Greek MS. of any kind is here offered. Under these circumstances it seems to *us* perfectly useless to continue negotiations with Mr Fenwick any longer.

This view was shared by Nicholson so far as the large transaction was concerned. In a letter to Thompson of 23 November he formally declined Fenwick's offer on behalf of the University and added:

My own view is that it would be better to drop joint action (letting Fenwick know that his prices have killed it) and that the three libraries should come to an understanding among themselves as to what classes of MSS. each should negotiate for separately.... There is another course open to us—to drop negotiations altogether and trust to Fenwick going to auction. This would be immeasurably the better plan if we could be sure that some American millionaire would not step in beforehand and buy the MSS. we need.

And thus the matter remained, though Thompson and Nicholson each made one more fruitless overture to Fenwick. In March 1891 the period set upon the transaction by the Treasury expired and the special grant to the Museum of £10,000 was automatically rescinded. In October of the same year at Oxford Convocation withdrew the £5000 which it had placed at the disposal of the Curators of the Bodleian, in spite of a plea by Nicholson to the Vice-Chancellor that the sum might remain available to be spent at auctions.

I have perhaps devoted more space to this time-consuming fiasco than it merits, but the reasons for the failure are worthy of analysis. The operation was, I think, too ambitious. Had one institution negotiated for a single group of manuscripts there would have been a greater chance of success. There are times, moreover, when the payment of a figure above the current market price can be justified, but whereas Thompson might have persuaded his own Trustees that this was in the ultimate public interest, the inclusion of the two University libraries made any such course trebly difficult. There is indeed no evidence to show that Thompson ever contemplated improving upon the conservative valuation placed upon the manuscripts by his own experts, for in my view the Museum's figure of £2800 for the 470 Latin classics was a low one, though not absurdly so. Fenwick's price of £7150 was certainly stiff, and was very high indeed compared with the £14,000 which he had asked and secured for the 621 Meerman manuscripts in the previous year. In fact the figures which Fenwick quoted to the Museum seem to me to be less generous than any of his offers to foreign institutions. I have not seen the correspondence exchanged between Thompson and Fenwick but it may well be that the two men found each other antipathetic. There is some evidence to show that Thompson was Olympian and autocratic in manner: certainly anything in the nature of haggling would have been distasteful to him. Perhaps the patronizing manner in which he wrote to Nicholson of 'young Fenwick' (who was thirty-four and Thompson fifty) was apparent to the vendor. Fenwick for his part never allowed any consideration of the national interest to interfere with his determination to secure the best possible price for his wares. The Phillipps Library was the Fenwick patrimony, and was only to be realized to the best possible advantage. The main factor, however, which must have influenced Thompson in breaking off negotiations was the strong likelihood that large parts of the collection would ultimately be sold at auction. This assumption was of course justified, and through purchases at public sales large numbers of the most valuable Phillipps manuscripts passed in due course into the possession of the British Museum, the Bodleian and, to a lesser degree, Cambridge University Library.[1]

[1] Fenwick's files relating to these abortive negotiations do not seem to have survived and my account is mainly derived from the relevant Library Papers at the Bodleian, for access to which I am indebted to Dr R. W. Hunt. See also Craster, *op. cit.* pp. 195–7.

1886–1914

Before embarking upon an account of the auction-sales of Phillipps books and manuscripts which took place at Sotheby's before the First World War, there are four private transactions of the same period which must be recorded. On 6 August 1886 a firm of Sheffield solicitors, Messrs Younge, Wilson and Co., wrote to Fenwick to ascertain on behalf of one of the partners, Charles Macro Wilson, whether the rich collection of Yorkshire topographical manuscripts formed by John Wilson of Broomhead Hall (1719–83) was likely to come on to the market. Charles Macro Wilson was a great-grandson of the original collector, and having antiquarian interests and a sense of family piety was anxious to recover the papers, which Phillipps had bought after an auction held in Sheffield in 1843. Negotiations proceeded at a leisurely pace and it was not until nine years later that Wilson and his brother visited Thirlestaine House. Fenwick had experienced considerable difficulty in reassembling the papers, which had been widely dispersed throughout the library. Eventually however, aided by a catalogue provided by the Wilson brothers, he was able, on 29 January 1896, to offer the whole collection, nearly five hundred manuscripts in number, to Charles Macro Wilson for fifteen hundred pounds, a price which the latter described as a very high one. Nevertheless early in February he re-examined the manuscripts in company with his brother and nephew, and agreed to buy them, and in April the collection was transferred from Cheltenham to Wilson's house, Waldershaigh, Bolsterstone, Sheffield. The Wilson family retained them in their possession until 1953 when Mr R. Macro Wilson sold them, through the agency of Mr Alan Keen, to the late C. K. Ogden.

Passing over the sale of a small group of Masonic manuscripts in 1900,[1] one more major disposal of topographical material remains to be noted, arranged by Prince Frederick Duleep Singh, who was keenly interested in the history and antiquities of East Anglia. The Prince visited Thirlestaine House in 1908 and was greatly struck by the value and size of the collections relating to Suffolk, which he brought to the notice of Lord Iveagh of Elveden Hall in that county. Lord Iveagh asked Duleep Singh to tell Fenwick that he would be disposed to buy the whole collection at a fair price. 'We should require a *good* price, but not a *fancy* one', replied Fenwick on 10 June 1908, and promised to prepare a list for the purchaser's consideration. This took a great deal longer than was anticipated, and it was not until July 1914 that Duleep Singh, accompanied by the Rev. Edmund Farrer, paid another visit to Cheltenham to inspect the whole collection on Lord Iveagh's behalf, and subsequently gave him a report on it. 'Mr Farrer and I went to see Lord Iveagh this morning', wrote Duleep Singh to Fenwick on 18 July 1914. 'He was somewhat staggered at the vastness of your Suffolk collections and—incidentally—at the price (roughly) that he would have to pay to acquire them. However I am glad to say he is not really averse to the idea.' Fenwick duly made a computation of their value and on 21 July 1914 he offered the collection to Lord Iveagh for £3750, a figure which was accepted by return of post.

The whole group comprised about seven hundred and fifty manuscripts bearing Phillipps numbers, but this figure hardly gives a true impression of its size. For whereas occasionally a Phillipps number was attached to a single deed, in other cases it might relate to a collection of papers bound in twenty-four volumes or to a long series of court-rolls. It must indeed have been one of the most important groups of topographical docu-

[1] To George W. Bain, Tunstall View, Ashbrooke Rd., Sunderland, for fifty-five guineas.

ments ever to have changed hands *en bloc*: for Phillipps had bought avidly at the sales of earlier collectors of Suffolk material, especially at those of Craven Ord and William Stevenson Fitch.

Two important sales to John Pierpont Morgan I (1837–1913) are unfortunately not documented by any correspondence among Fenwick's papers. In 1905 or 1906 the American collector acquired a group of five manuscripts in elaborate medieval bindings decorated with silver, precious stones, ivory or enamel (16396, 16411, 16400, 16387, 16388= Morgan MSS. 561–565). All these had been bought by Phillipps at the Libri sale of 1862, and although the manuscripts themselves are by no means negligible and the components of the bindings for the most part medieval in date, subsequent study and general recognition of the scale of the unscrupulous Libri's *remboîtages* and fabrications have long made it impossible to accept four of the bindings as entities of an early period. No such qualified praise however needs to be applied to Morgan's purchase in 1911 of one of the great treasures of Italian illumination, the late eleventh-century Gospels given by Matilda, Countess of Tuscany, to the Benedictines of Polirone, near Mantua, in 1097 (3500: Morgan MS. 492). The price at which this famous volume changed hands was £8000. So well pleased was the collector with his purchase that he chose the volume as the subject of a monograph for presentation to his fellow-members of the Roxburghe Club, and, although his death intervened, Sir George Warner's account of the manuscript was presented to the Club in 1917 by Morgan's son in fulfilment of his father's wish.

These transactions with private individuals, together with those carried out with institutional purchasers described in the preceding chapter, produced over £56,000. Up to the year 1914 Fenwick also held sixteen auction-sales of Phillipps material at Sotheby's, which in their turn added a total of £71,277 to the receipts. Unfortunately no correspondence between Fenwick and Messrs Sotheby has come to light and my account of the sales has therefore had to be based almost solely upon my examination of a set of the priced catalogues. The problem of how to construct a readable narrative from a string of lots and prices has proved insoluble, and I earnestly advise all but the most hardened enthusiasts for sale-room history to skip the next few pages.

Close reading of the catalogues prompts one or two general reflections. Fenwick not only made the selection of manuscripts but wrote the descriptions himself, descriptions which compare well with that period's standards of auction-cataloguing although to our eyes they are too highly tinged with promotional hyperbole. Whereas Fenwick sold privately blocks of manuscripts which had some homogeneity, he took great pains in making up the auction-sales to sell balanced cross-sections of the whole collection. He was indeed an extraordinarily astute watcher of the market, keenly alive to the dangers of flooding it with too large groups of similar material, nor did he ever allow any consideration to deflect him from securing the best possible price. The dispersal all over the world of groups of historical material such as the Southwell or the Macartney papers was a matter for lament by scholars, but Fenwick decided, and probably rightly, that such collections would realize more if they were sold in a number of small lots than *en bloc*. Occasionally even medieval books containing two or more texts from the same scriptorium were divided and sold separately. 'I hope you will not mind my writing to ask', inquired Francis Jenkinson on 5 June 1898, 'whether you have the rest of the volume which is lot 100 in this sale. It seems a cruel severance....' 'I cannot help thinking', he added in the same letter, 'that in the case of charters your method defeats its own object. A person may be interested in a Cornish manor: but in your catalogue he finds the documents relating to that manor scattered thro' many lots. No doubt you hope he will bid for them all—but it is equally probable that he will give it up and bid for none. In my own case 141, 142, 143 [Cambridge deeds] are no use separately; & if I lose one I shall not bid at all for the others.' Fenwick however knew his own business best, and his policy, regrettable from a scholarly standpoint, of splitting the manuscripts into the largest possible number of lots certainly paid financial dividends. Few libraries have ever been more effectively dispersed, and one must admire the restraint with which Fenwick refrained from putting too great a share of the cream of the collection on to the market at any one time. The greatest treasures indeed, particularly first-class illuminated manu-scripts with miniatures,[1] he never sold by auction at all.

The following table gives an analysis of the auction-sales which took place before the First World War, and to avoid wearisome repetition of dates, the roman numerals preceding each entry will be used as references in the text to individual sales.

i.	3–10 August 1886	3346 lots	printed books	£2200. 15s. 0d.
ii.	22–4 January 1889	1413 lots	printed books	637. 17s. 0d.
iii.	15–16 July 1891	542 lots	autograph letters	891. 11s. 6d.
iv.	7–8 December 1891	703 lots	printed books	371. 1s. 6d.
v.	4–6 July 1892	601 lots	autograph letters	720. 1s. 6d.
vi.	19–22 June 1893	915 lots	MSS.	2474. 4s. 0d.
vii.	21–6 March 1895	1285 lots	MSS.	8468. 2s. 0d.
viii.	10–17 June 1896	1441 lots	MSS.	6998. 7s. 0d.
ix.	17–20 May 1897	826 lots	MSS.	4194. 14s. 6d.
x.	6–11 June 1898	1168 lots	MSS.	5915. 18s. 0d.
xi.	5–10 June 1899	1258 lots	MSS.	3784. 19s. 6d.
xii.	27 April–2 May 1903	1355 lots	MSS.	4612. 4s. 0d.
xiii.	15–18 June 1908	835 lots	MSS.	3796. 19s. 0d.
xiv.	6–9 June 1910	908 lots	MSS.	5959. 11s. 6d.
xv.	24–8 April 1911	1143 lots	MSS.	8795. 17s. 6d.
xvi.	19–23 May 1913	1137 lots	MSS.	11454. 18s. 0d.
		18876		£71277. 1s. 6d.

The three early sales of duplicate printed books (Nos. i, ii and iv) contained comparatively little of major interest. Two *editiones principes* call for mention, the Sussex copy of the Fust and Schoeffer Cicero's *De officiis*, 1465 (i, 1047) which fetched £58, and Pliny's *Naturalis Historiae Libri XXXVII*, Venice, Johannes de Spira, 1469 (i, 2823, £36). Sale No. iv contained many minor incunabula,

---

[1] Of which an important account by Comte Paul Durrieu is to be found in *Bibliothèque de l'École des Chartes*, L (1889), pp. 381–432. The illuminated Meerman manuscripts were the subject of a special monograph by Joachim Kirchner, *Beschreibendes Verzeichnis der Miniaturen und des Initialschmuckes in den Phillipps-Handschriften* (Leipzig, 1926).

few of which realized as much as a pound. The opportunity was taken to include long runs of Sir Thomas Phillipps's own privately printed works (e.g. i, 2389–2514) which had proved so difficult to market in the great collector's own lifetime. Fenwick had already in 1886 printed a catalogue[1] of these books and had sold a good many of them through the agency of Quaritch: a few years later Henry Gray, who traded at the Genealogical Record Office and Bookstore, East Acton, was also active in selling them. Some of the prices realized at auction would have gratified Sir Thomas: *Monumental Inscriptions in the County of Wilton*, 1822, fetched £14. 10s. (i, 2436); £16 was paid for the massive *Collectanea de familiis diversis quibus nomen est Phillipps* (i, 2501); and £15. 15s. for a copy of Bigland's *Historical Collections relative to the County of Gloucester*, 1791–92, with the additions to the work printed privately by Phillipps and after his death by Fenwick (i, 793).

The two sales of autograph letters (Nos. iii and v) contained many desirable items, among them a letter of Sir Thomas Bodley to Constantine Huyghens (iii, 43, £54), two letters from Chatterton to Dodsley (iii, 101, £20 and v, 201, £30), Defoe (iii, 133, £46), four original letters of Junius (iii, 283, £130), a six-page letter from Livingstone on African exploration (v, 410, £2. 12s. 6d.), Shakespeare's Sir Thomas Lucy (iii, 322, £28), Newton to Pepys on the odds in dicing (v, 450, £40), two letters from Dean Swift (iii, 474, £40 and v, 549, £26). The sale of 1892 contained a large group of letters of American interest (v, 13–115) mostly bought by Sabin for modest sums. A letter of Benjamin Franklin, for example, cost him £2. 6s. (v, 38) and £7. 5s. secured an important letter of George Washington (v, 111).

On 19 June 1893 the sales of the manuscripts proper began. This sale (No. vi) contained no manuscripts earlier than the fifteenth century, and for the most part comprised historical, topographical

---

[1] *The Middle Hill Press: a short Catalogue of some of Sir Thomas Phillipps' privately printed Works*, pp. 12, J. Davy and Sons, Dryden Press, 137 Long Acre, London, 1886.

and literary papers, some of them of considerable bulk. Thirty-nine folio volumes of Basil Montagu's collections relating to the life and works of Lord Bacon fetched a mere ten shillings (vi, 21); the Bodleian Library secured through Quaritch for £17 thirteen volumes of Philip Bliss's antiquarian papers (vi, 47) and a similar number of volumes of John Britton's papers fetched £8. 5s. (vi, 56). Fenwick bought in for £41 in the name of Maine seventy-nine volumes of John Caley's transcripts and indexes of public records, which had cost Phillipps upwards of £500 in 1834. The most expensive lot in the sale was No. 734, the original manuscript of Walter Scott's Life of Swift (7294), for which Quaritch paid the astonishing sum of £230 on behalf of the American collector, Robert Hoe.[1] Many of the most valuable items were secured by Quaritch for the British Museum, among them a large volume of Sir Julius Caesar's papers for £75 (9111: vi, 75),[2] a fine manuscript of poems by Chaucer, Lydgate and others (9053: vi, 122, £100),[3] and the volumes of greatest historical interest among the Southwell and Blathwayte State Papers and correspondence, which Fenwick had lotted separately (vi, 767–839).

The seventh sale, which began on 21 March 1895, contained a higher proportion of early manuscripts on vellum. It was also notable for the emergence of a new large-scale trade buyer, H. S. Nichols of 62A Piccadilly, who outbid Quaritch for nearly all the major items. He paid £135. 9s. for lot 69, a thirteenth-century metrical life of Thomas à Becket (11753),[4] £129 for lot 131, a collection of legal texts of the same period (8078),[5] £94, £140 and £130 for lots 281, 385 and 297 respectively, Wardrobe Books of Edward III, 1332 (3786), Henry VIII, 1531–32 (3614), and Elizabeth I, 1559–60 (4092).[6] A number of fine twelfth-century books sold for between £15 and £30, and several signed and dated Renaissance manuscripts fetched what we would now regard as very modest sums indeed. One may instance a text of

---

[1] Resold in Hoe sale 1912, lot 3002, to Rosenbach for $1910.
[2] B.M. Add. MS. 34324.   [3] B.M. Add. MS. 34360.
[4] B.M. Add. MS. 35180.   [5] B.M. Add. MS. 35179.
[6] B.M. Add. MSS. 35181, 35182 and 35185.

Sedulius on vellum dated 1455 (119: vii, 1016, £2. 19s.), and Michael Savonarola's 'De balneis et thermis naturalibus', also on vellum, 1442 (14878: vii, 964, £4);[1] a few classical manuscripts aroused greater competition. A Catullus of 1453 (9591: vii, 141)[2] realized £35, and a Vergil of 1474 £22 (4585: vii, 1136).[3] In general, contemporary opinion regarded the prices as very high.

I hope you were content with your last sale [wrote Warner to Fenwick on 10 April 1895]. You certainly ought to be, and Nichols merits a hand and a commission. I am curious to see *his* catalogue when it appears.

I suppose, as you say, one ought to be well satisfied with the result [replied Fenwick on 28 April] & though Nichols was a great help, I cannot by any means say that his success was entirely due to his presence. Instead of my giving him a commission I think he ought to give me one for affording him an opportunity of bringing his name so prominently before the public!! Do you really think he bought all the MSS. for stock? I can hardly believe it & fancy that he must have been buying at least some on commission.

The high prices were also a matter for comment by William Morris in a letter of 23 March 1895 to F. S. Ellis.

As the history of sales seems to interest you [he wrote], hear a tale of the Phillipps sale, of which today is the third day. Two books I bid for. A 13th century Aristotelian book [4252: lot 28][4] with three very pretty initials, but imperfect top and tail. I put £15 on this with many misgivings as to my folly—hi! it fetched £50!! A really pretty little book, Gregory's Decretals [5303: lot 358], with four or five very tiny illuminations; I took a fancy to it and put £40 on it, expecting to get it for £25—ho!! it fetched £96!!! Rejoice with me that I have got 82 Mss., as clearly I shall never get another.[5]

Morris's gloomy prognostications were not fulfilled, for at the next Phillipps sale, beginning on 10 June 1896, he bought two

---

[1] Bibliothèque Nationale n.a. Lat. 889.
[2] Bodleian MS. Lat. class. e. 17.
[3] Princeton University Library.
[4] Cambridge, Fitzwilliam, McClean 156.
[5] J. W. Mackail, *Life of William Morris*, II, p. 311.

manuscripts. He gave Quaritch a commission of £150 to buy lot 609, a finely written Hegesippus of the twelfth century in a contemporary stamped binding, which the bookseller secured for the trifling sum of £13. Quaritch also bought for Morris at £34 a very fine twelfth-century English service book with two hundred large initials (viii, 978). The absence of Nichols's competition made for less buoyant bidding and there were some distinct bargains even by the standards of those days of greater opportunity. A twelfth-century Augustine with a monastic provenance cannot be regarded as anything but cheap at £6 (14917: viii, 44), and a fifteenth-century Catullus at £7. 7s. 0d. (3364: viii, 189)[1] hardly reflects the rarity of that author's manuscripts in commerce; £2. 11s. 0d. secured a life of St Margaret, an English manuscript on vellum of the fifteenth century (9227: viii, 852),[2] an English verse miscellany of the same date, also on vellum, brought only £5. 5s. (18134: viii, 965),[3] and among the earlier manuscripts a heavily glossed Priscian of the eleventh century changed hands at £7 (2974: viii, 975),[4] while double that sum sufficed to buy in a collection of tracts by Anselm and others of the same date with fine initials and in a contemporary binding (2329: viii, 11).[5]

Apart from Morris and other private collectors such as H. H. Bemrose of Irongate, Derby, Quaritch was also buying for the British Museum, Cambridge University Library, the Bodleian and for Harrasowitz, the bookseller who in his turn was acting for the Prussian State Library. Quaritch's purchases included an Elizabethan Wardrobe Book, 1568–89 (8853: viii, 459, £100),[6] a tenth-century copy of John Chrysostom on St John's Gospel (16394: viii, 503, £69),[7] a very fine text of Henry of Huntingdon of the beginning of the fourteenth century (8079: viii, 610),[8] a

---

[1] Bodleian MS. Lat. class. e. 15.   [2] Bodleian MS. Eng. th. e. 18.
[3] Wellcome Historical Medical Museum MS. 1510.
[4] Harvard University Library.
[5] Resold (xii, 27) for £45; Berlin Theol. Qu. 319.
[6] B.M. MS. Egerton 2806.
[7] Berlin Theol. Lat. F. 587.
[8] Cambridge University Library MS. Add. 3392.

sixteenth-century poetical miscellany containing among others the works of Surrey and Wyatt (9474: viii, 1206, £40. 10s.)[1] and a noble eleventh-century manuscript of the New Testament with Bede's commentary, containing historiated initials, some of them nearly twelve inches long (11825: viii, 1240, £120).[2] The first day's sale was enlivened by the presence of a private collector, Frank McClean, F.R.S. (1837–1904), whose determined bidding secured a number of lots which he subsequently bequeathed to the Fitzwilliam Museum, Cambridge (viii, 85, 112, 128, 129, 131, 136, 139 and 172).

From the owner's point of view the ninth sale, which began on 17 May 1897, was less successful, and Fenwick bought many lots in under such fictitious names as Sandford, Blythstein, Maitland, Snell, Beaumont, Oxburgh, Little, Rogers, T. Smith and Waring. He let go however for almost nothing several very large lots of Phillipps's sale catalogues. About five hundred, for example, issued by Puttick and Simpson and their predecessors realized three shillings (ix, 87), while fourteen shillings sufficed to buy six hundred and fifty catalogues of the house of Sotheby from 1784 onwards (ix, 92) and a florin secured nearly two hundred and thirty of Evans (ix, 95): all these were bought by William Roberts (1862–1940), art correspondent to *The Times* and author of several well-known works on bookselling and book-collecting. A fifteenth-century manuscript of Pomponius Mela and Solinus, written by two named scribes, failed to attract a single bid (3363: ix, 614),[3] a volume containing eight printed Shakespeare quartos, five of them imperfect, was bought in for £170 (ix, 691) and a very extensive collection of R. B. Sheridan's correspondence was certainly cheap at £13 (18472, 18504: ix, 702, Quaritch). Also very cheap, and bought by the same bookseller, was the manuscript of the letters of St Jerome and St Augustine in a very fine

[1] B.M. Add. MS. 36529.
[2] Manchester, John Rylands MS. Lat. 107.
[3] Reoffered x, 855 and again bought in; sold xii, 296, Bibliothèque Nationale n.a. Lat. 783.

stamped fifteenth-century binding (9655: ix, 395, £30) which was subsequently illustrated as the frontispiece of the late E. P. Goldschmidt's *Gothic and Renaissance Bookbindings*, and is now in the Pierpont Morgan Library.

The next sale (6 June 1898) contained some important manuscripts such as sixteen letters of John Dryden bought by Sabin for £330 on behalf of Pierpont Morgan (21867: x, 313), a volume of correspondence including eight autograph letters from Oliver Cromwell, relating to the siege of Pontefract (8747: x, 401, £415, Downing), a cartulary of Fountains Abbey (11122: x, 592, £155),[1] a fourteenth-century manuscript in English of metrical lives of the saints (8253: x, 934, £111, Quaritch)[2] and a celebrated unique fifteenth-century text on vellum of *The Sowdon of Babylone* for which Quaritch paid £60 and which passed into the collection of Robert Garrett of Baltimore (8357: x, 976). Among other buyers are to be found Francis Jenkinson bidding in person on behalf of Cambridge University Library, and young Mr S. C. Cockerell (later Sir Sydney), who was already making a number of modest but highly discriminating purchases.

At the eleventh sale (5 June 1899) again a good deal was bought in or sold for very small sums. Dobell secured for £2 the papers of Sir Egerton Brydges bound in forty-nine volumes (xi, 267–273);[3] fourteen volumes of the papers of Sir John Chardin, the traveller, were bought in for only six shillings (xi, 333) and Pickering laid out ten shillings well upon lot 452, a volume of ninety letters of authors addressed to Robert Dodsley. Even eighty-one autograph letters of Leibnitz changed hands for £39 (23693: xi, 813, Quaritch) and the manuscript catalogue of Horace Walpole's library at Strawberry Hill (11792: xi, 1173)[4] realized £3. A cartulary of Byland brought £63 (13843: xi, 1238), a price which compares very favourably with the £307

---

[1] Bought by Sir Thomas Brooke; now B.M. Add. MS. 37770.
[2] B.M. MS. Egerton 2810.
[3] Subsequently in Michael Sadleir's library.
[4] In the library of Lord Walpole of Wolterton.

which the Belgian Government had to pay to secure a fine thirteenth-century cartulary of the Benedictine House of St Lambert at Liessies (8839: xi, 821).

On 27 April 1903 the twelfth sale began. Autograph letters of David Garrick (34993: xii, 491) and Charles Lamb (34973: xii, 678) sold reasonably well at £10. 15s. and £24. 10s. respectively, but on the whole prices give the impression that palates both of the trade and of private collectors were becoming jaded at the series of rich feasts which had been laid before them at frequent intervals during the previous decade. Sir Sydney Cockerell made half a dozen purchases at prices which ranged between twenty-five pounds and twenty-seven shillings, the latter sum being paid for an Italian fifteenth-century manuscript on vellum of the *De gestis Romanorum* of Hercules Brunus and other tracts (8074: xii, 190), a book which illustrates neatly the thesis that for over a century Renaissance manuscripts showed not the slightest appreciation in value. In 1785 at the sale of Anthony Askew's manuscripts it realized sixteen shillings and passed into the possession of Michael Wodhull. He however discarded it and Richard Heber bought it for six shillings and sixpence. At the sale of Heber's manuscripts in 1836 it fetched ten shillings and passed into the Phillipps Collection. Fenwick first put it into the Phillipps sale of 1899 when he bought it in for fourteen shillings (xi, 710), but placed it in the next sale, where Sir Sydney secured it for only eleven shillings more than it realized in the Askew sale one hundred and sixteen years before. A greater bargain passed through the auction-room on this occasion, the true worth of which was unrecognized by the seller, the auctioneer or the buyer. A fourteenth-century text on vellum of Valerius Maximus was bought by Dobell for the price, reasonable by comparison with similar material, of £2. 15s. 0d. (2714: xii, 1149). This volume, now in Harvard University Library, was subsequently shown to be Petrarch's own annotated copy.

Fenwick allowed five years to elapse before making a further trial of the market, but at the thirteenth sale (15 June 1908) prices do not seem to have materially advanced. Many twelfth-century manuscripts changed hands for around ten pounds, and a further selection from the Southwell papers, again lotted separately (xiii, 684–699), sold for very small sums. The total of the sale which followed, however (6 June 1910), was raised by a number of three-figure lots, among them a cartulary of Beverley for which B. F. Stevens paid £138 on behalf of the Library of Congress (11915: xiv, 902); Quaritch gave £140 for the original treaty of marriage, dated 1364, between Edward Duke of York, fifth son of Edward III, and Margaret, Duchess of Burgundy (27729: xiv, 283). This seems to be a substantial price, but it was eclipsed by the £520 which Charles Fairfax Murray, bidding against Quaritch, paid for Phillipps MS. No. 6358 (xiv, 809), the original treaty, written on fifteen sheets of vellum, which put an end to the war of Chioggia, 1378–81, a document, signed at Turin on 8 August 1381, of cardinal importance in the history of Venice. Other substantial prices included £86 paid for a further group of fifty-one autograph letters in the hand of Leibnitz (1170: xiv, 503, Quaritch), and £50, a large sum at that date, for a poetical miscellany of the time of Charles I which contained much of the work of Thomas Randolph (13187: xiv, 672).[1] At this sale many lots, especially charters, were acquired by the John Rylands Library, which was also a heavy buyer at the next dispersal (24 April 1911), when through Quaritch it paid £505 for a cartulary of St Mary's, York (8135: xv, 1132), a price which is likely to have been a record for a cartulary at that date. It had cost Phillipps £155 at the Heber sale in 1836. Several other important lots passed to the Rylands Library, including a cartulary of the Cistercian house of Wardon, Bedfordshire (21708: xv, 1084, £172). Another cartulary fetched a substantial sum, that of Forde Abbey, for which Phillipps had paid £100 in 1847, and which was now sold for £235 (13823: xv, 386).[2] Another medieval manuscript on vellum deserves mention, the unique text

[1] Harvard University Library.
[2] The property of G. D. Roper, Esq., Forde Abbey.

of *The Rule of the Christian Religion* by Reginald Pecock, Bishop of Chichester (6243: xv, 801, £151).[1]

The final sale to be held before the First World War (19 May 1913) was notable for the inclusion of a very large block of *Americana* (xvi, 13–511) for which the firms of Henry Stevens, B. F. Stevens, Sabin, Hiersemann and Quaritch eagerly competed. The celebrated manuscript of Richard Hakluyt's memorandum on the advantages likely to accrue to England by the 'westerne discoveries lately attempted' was secured by Henry Stevens for £215 for the New York Public Library (14097: xvi, 43), and Quaritch paid £360 for seven folio ledgers of the Commissioners investigating the losses of the loyalists in the American War of Independence (24424: xvi, 68). Among medieval manuscripts of interest were a fifteenth-century volume of metrical homilies and tales from the north of England for which Maggs paid £145 (8122: xvi, 1008), and an album containing 210 fragments of manuscripts from the eighth to the fifteenth century, bought by Barnard for £60 (15758: xvi, 742) and sold by him to Sir Sydney Cockerell.[2] At this sale Fenwick let go for £59 Phillipps's expensively purchased Caley collections (xvi, 572) which he had bought in for £41 in 1893.

It will readily be understood that the work of selecting and cataloguing material for these sixteen auctions and for the many substantial private sales occupied a great deal of Fenwick's time. His father, John Fenwick, had died in May 1903, while his mother, Katharine, Sir Thomas's last surviving child, died at the age of ninety on 4 June 1913. Older members of the family still remember with affection the small old lady of great sweetness of disposition who presided at Thirlestaine House.[3] She did not lack strength of character, and being her father's daughter, she unfortunately could not give her unqualified approval to Fenwick's

[1] Pierpont Morgan Library MS. 519.

[2] Resold for £850 by Sir Sydney Cockerell at Sotheby's, 3 April 1957, lot 2.

[3] She makes a brief appearance in an interesting account of Thirlestaine House in Mrs Susan Hicks Beach's *The Yesterdays behind the Door* (Liverpool University Press, 1956).

marriage in 1905 to a Roman Catholic, the widow of Sir Thomas Sidgreaves, Chief Justice of the Straits Settlements. This led Fenwick to buy a house at Sidmouth, where he and his wife spent part of the year, a circumstance which meant that at times there was considerable delay in replying to the numerous letters which scholars continued to address to the owner of Bibliotheca Phillippica.

Difficulty of access to the manuscripts—and at times access was very difficult indeed—was the main complaint which scholars made against Fenwick. Sometimes of course, failing to understand the peculiar history and circumstances of the establishment at Thirlestaine House, they made demands which were quite unreasonable when addressed to the owner of a private library. Fenwick, moreover, for his part often failed to appreciate the frustration which a scholar would feel if he were kept waiting for months for a sight of a manuscript vital to the completion of some laborious and unremunerative piece of research. The principles which governed admission to the library were simple. No visitor was ever admitted if Fenwick were away from home, and for large parts of 1903 and 1913, when he spent many months abroad, his absence imposed a complete ban on the use of the library. His plans too were often uncertain and after a month's delay an applicant might well receive a letter stating that he was away from Cheltenham and did not at present know the date of his return. When therefore Fenwick was at home a scholar was well advised to drop everything else and hurry to the library, a counsel of perfection not always capable of being carried out. 'You doubtless gathered from my letter that Literature was my only occupation but this is not so', wrote the Biblical scholar H. C. Hoskier on 30 July 1886. 'I am engaged in the City all day & every day & it is almost only on such occasions as Bank Holidays that I find myself free to pursue such an enquiry as the one I had set before myself with regard to your MSS. of evangelia & Acta apostolorum.' No manuscript was ever allowed to leave the house and any such arrangement therefore as the deposit of a book for a

65

period at the British Museum was out of the question. I have noted only a single exception to this rule, when in 1898 F. W. Maitland was ill at Stroud and Fenwick sent a servant to his bedside bearing a manuscript for collation. Photography was also banned, since Fenwick believed, sometimes mistakenly, that the reproduction of any part of a manuscript detracted from its cash value. In 1902 for example he even refused Henri Omont leave to reproduce part of MS. No. 8025 *bis* in a *Festschrift* in honour of Léopold Delisle, whose fruitful connexion with the library had extended for more than forty years. Very occasionally the rule forbidding photography was relaxed on the score of personal friendship. In 1912 for example S. G. Owen was favoured with a reproduction of two pages of a manuscript of Juvenal, and in 1896 Lord Crawford photographed a group of medieval jewelled bindings, sending Fenwick in return some of the catalogues of Bibliotheca Lindesiana.

If Fenwick were at home, however, three or four days' notice was sufficient to obtain entry. Strangers were required to furnish a reference from some institutional librarian, and access to the library was normally granted between the hours of ten and five. From 1902 onwards Fenwick used to state that the fee of one pound a day was given to charity. On occasions this was reduced to ten shillings in the case of scholars who pleaded poverty, and even in exceptional circumstances waived altogether. Too much must not be made of these difficulties. Many distinguished scholars contrived to pursue their studies at Cheltenham,[1] and to many others Fenwick returned courteous replies to postal

---

[1] Among distinguished visitors before 1914 I have noted the names of the following: Karl Bartsch, Carleton Brown, J. W. Burgon, H. J. Chaytor, Sir Sydney Cockerell, bringing in 1904 Henry Yates Thompson and in 1908 Mr Dyson Perrins; W. E. Crum, Comte Paul Durrieu, Mr H. W. Garrod, James Rendel Harris, H. C. Hoskier, A. E. Housman, M. R. James, A. G. Little, Paul Meyer, Theodor Mommsen, Dom Germain Morin, S. G. Owen, Reginald Lane Poole, Lucy Toulmin Smith and Heinrich Schenkl, who put other scholars in his debt by devoting a fascicule of his *Bibliotheca Patrum Latinorum Britannica* to the Phillipps collection (Vol. I, part ii, Vienna, 1892). On pp. 156–7 of this work he makes some severe strictures on the difficulty of consulting manuscripts at Cheltenham.

inquiries.[1] It did indeed take Mr H. W. Garrod six months, not to mention eleven letters and a telegram, to get a sight of a manuscript of Statius in 1904, but in his case, as in many others, patience, persistence and an ability to pay the fee were rewarded in the end.

[1] Among scholars' letters before 1914 preserved by Fenwick I have noted examples from Lord Acton, P. S. Allen, W. A. Baillie-Grohman, Ingram Bywater, Paul Fabre, Cesare Foligno, C. R. Gregory, Arthur Haseloff, A. M. Hind, Andrew Lang, W. M. Lindsay, John Livingston Lowes, H. R. Luard, W. D. Macray, Paul Marchegay, Edward Moore, Reinhold Pauli, J. P. Postgate, Hastings Rashdall, Seymour de Ricci, J. Armitage Robinson, W. H. D. Rouse, Sir George Sitwell, Alexander Souter and C. E. Stuart.

CHAPTER V

1916-1938

Two sales to John Pierpont Morgan II — transactions with Sir Chester Beatty — Dr A. S. W. Rosenbach's substantial purchases — acquisition of Irish MSS. by the National Library of Ireland — six auction-sales at Sotheby's, 1919–38 — Sir Walter Raleigh's commonplace book — the character of Thomas FitzRoy Fenwick — the author's visit to Thirlestaine House.

The sales to John Pierpont Morgan I which were recorded in the previous chapter found their counterpart in two transactions with his son, John Pierpont Morgan II (1867–1943), in which three manuscripts, two of them of the very highest quality and one remarkable for its binding, changed hands. Negotiations were carried out with considerable expertise by Belle da Costa Greene (d. 1950), Morgan's Librarian and Director of the Pierpont Morgan Library from its incorporation as a public institution in 1924 until her retirement in 1948. Miss Greene's vital personality, the verve, charm and flair with which she sought out accessions, made her a legend in her lifetime and were posthumously commemorated in a noble volume[1] in which scholars of many nationalities combined to honour her remarkable talents. Fenwick carefully preserved the records of his negotiations with her, and the present Director of the Morgan Library, Mr Frederick B. Adams, Junior, has kindly sent me extracts from the relevant documents in the Library's files.

On 8 November 1916 the well-known collector of manuscripts Henry Yates Thompson (1838–1928) wrote to Fenwick to ascertain whether he might bring Miss Greene down to Cheltenham. The visit duly took place on 21 November. The late E. P. Goldschmidt used to recall Miss Greene's account of how Fenwick

---

[1] *Studies in Art and Literature for Belle da Costa Greene*, edited by Dorothy Miner (Princeton, 1954).

showed her Phillipps MS. 8025 *bis* (now Morgan MS. 638), forty-three leaves of Old Testament illustrations containing eighty-six full-page miniatures of the finest Parisian workmanship of the thirteenth century. Fenwick's estimate of its value was £10,000 and Miss Greene was secretly amused at how obviously disconcerted the owner was when she closed the deal with an eager and instantaneous acceptance of this figure. It was indeed a great prize, not only for the quality of illumination, but also for the romantic migrations which it had undergone; for in 1604 Cardinal Bernard Maciejowski sent it as a present to the King of Persia, Shah-Abbas the Great, who caused to be written in the margins captions in Persian describing each miniature. It will be recalled that Robert Curzon made an unavailing attempt to buy this manuscript from Phillipps in 1869.[1] Two other leaves from the book are in the Bibliothèque Nationale (nouv. acq. lat. 2294) and one other was until 1957 in the possession of Sir Sydney Cockerell,[2] who published a description of the whole manuscript in 1927 for the Roxburghe Club. On 21 November Miss Greene wrote to Fenwick asking him to keep the purchase and the price secret, and three days later she sent a formal letter to be laid before the Court of Chancery, which authorized the sale on 1 December.

On 27 March 1920 Miss Greene wrote proposing another visit to Cheltenham, asking to examine manuscripts dating from before the fourteenth century. 'Do you object to my asking you not to let anyone know of my visit?' she wrote. 'It will be infinitely and *mutually* better so.'[3] She arrived on 8 April, and drafts of two

---

[1] See *Phillipps Studies*, no. 4, pp. 154–5.

[2] The leaf was sold to the New York bookseller, H. P. Kraus, in 1957. Sir Sydney, whose advice and encouragement have been lavished upon collectors of manuscripts for more than sixty years, told me that it had been his hope that Yates Thompson himself would have bought the manuscript, and that at the time Sir Sydney felt that Yates Thompson had made a tactical error in escorting Miss Greene to Cheltenham and allowing her to carry off the prize from under his nose.

[3] At least one bookseller had been urging his claims upon Miss Greene that he was the most suitable and indeed the only agent to conduct negotiations with Fenwick on her behalf. She subsequently took pleasure, not totally unmalicious, in announcing her unaided success.

letters to Morgan give a glimpse of the subsequent negotiation. The two most important manuscripts left at Cheltenham were, she said, Phillipps MS. 21975, the famous tenth-century Dioscorides[1] with numerous illustrations (now Morgan MS. 652), and 3007, an eleventh-century copy of the Gospels, written at Cologne, and contained in an important medieval binding with ivory plaques (now Morgan MS. 651). Fenwick's price was £13,000 for the two and she did not discuss this figure with him. 'When I first took the Dioscorides off the shelf', she added, 'my eye hit upon a note inserted at the flyleaf saying that the German Government through someone (whose name I cannot recall) of Berlin had offered 9,500 pounds for the two books in 1912...before I had a chance to look further, he called my attention to something else. When I returned to the Dioscorides the slip containing this note had been removed! Funny?'

The further progress of the transaction is chronicled in a flight of telegrams, the first from Rome dated 7 May 1920.

Just received cable Morgan cannot give price you ask authorises me to offer ten thousand pounds cash knowing market value of such manuscripts consider this very fine offer and more than at auction in view of future business hope you accept telegraph reply Ritz Hotel Paris sailing Adriatic twelfth.

BELLE DA COSTA GREENE

So surprised and disappointed at price offered [ran Fenwick's reply] considering the importance and condition of the works but would ask the sanction of the Court if Mr M. would make price eleven thousand. Can I see you before you leave England.

Yours just received [telegraphed Miss Greene from Paris on 10 May]. Chief's offer based on knowledge of market and recent purchases always exceptionally just especially in private negotiations. Think could realise this. Will take personally responsibility of making offer ten thousand five hundred as anxious to close transaction but cannot do more. Appreciate both your disappointment and cooperation regret cannot see you as sailing from Cherbourg please write or telegraph me

---

[1] See *Phillipps Studies*, no. 4, pp. 78–80.

your decision care of steamship Adriatic leaving Southampton twelfth hope understand there will be no break in our friendly relations even if your decision is against us.

In an answer written the same day Fenwick once more urged Miss Greene to place before Morgan various factors which in the owner's view justified the higher figure, but on 15 July she wrote that after discussion in New York no advance could be made. 'I consider Mr Morgan's final offer to be not only just but *high*,' she asserted, 'and would ask you to let either Mr Morgan or myself have your decision in regard to selling them at this price (£10,500) before August 15th. Mr Morgan does not wish to keep his offer open after that date.'

Fenwick having resigned himself to the acceptance of the lower figure had in fact already secured the Court's permission to sell, and, during an agreeable meeting in London in August, he handed over the two precious accessions to Morgan in person.

Barely had this substantial transaction been concluded when Fenwick embarked on a larger series of private sales. Alfred Chester Beatty (b. 1875, since 1954 Sir Chester Beatty) has devoted to the arts and to the promotion of scholarship a liberal share of the fortune acquired from his world-wide mining interests. Students of papyri and of Western and Oriental manuscripts have reason to be grateful to him not only for the series of scholarly catalogues which he has commissioned, but also for the hospitable welcome which is extended to scholars visiting the Chester Beatty Library in Dublin.

In October 1920 Fenwick asked the advice of Sir Chester, who did not exchange his American for British citizenship until 1933, on the possibility of the sale of a large block of manuscripts to the Boston Museum of Fine Arts or some other American institution. Two months later Sir Chester, who already owned a number of manuscripts, suggested that he should visit Cheltenham with a view to making some purchases on his own account. He arrived on 14 December and was joined at Thirlestaine House by his wife. Both enjoyed Fenwick's hospitality and during the visit Sir Chester agreed to buy twenty-four manuscripts and two fragments for the sum of £11,954. Of these the most notable were No. 2165= 21787, a ninth-century Franco-Saxon Gospels,[1] No. 4259, a splendid folio Bible of the thirteenth century in four volumes,[2] No. 4769, a twelfth-century Bible from Walsingham Priory with part of a contemporary rental of that foundation bound in,[3] and No. 12348, a finely decorated Gospels from Stavelot Abbey written about A.D. 1000.[4]

The books were collected on 31 December 1920 and Fenwick wrote ruefully to the new owner on the same day.

Alas! the books have just gone, and one more chapter in their history is closed—a long chapter indeed—for many of them have been for close on a hundred years in the family possession. The New Year will find them in a new home, where I am convinced they will be appreciated to the fullest extent by two such devotees to medieval art as your charming wife and yourself. May they bring you an immense amount of present pleasure, and in wishing you both a happy New Year may I express a hope that they will for many years to come be a source of enjoyment, instruction and entertainment to yourselves and your friends. Parting with old friends is always painful, but having lived with them from boyhood I have had a long innings so must not grudge them going into other hands.

In the spring of 1921 Sir Chester proposed a further visit but circumstances conspired to delay it until 1923, for throughout 1921 Fenwick's first wife was seriously ill at his house in Sidmouth and after her death in 1922 he travelled extensively. When in February 1923 the long-postponed meeting was at last arranged Sir Chester warned Fenwick that high taxation would tend to reduce his purchasing capacity.

'Please do not let that in any way make you hesitate about paying me a visit,' replied Fenwick on 9 February 1923, 'for apart

[1] E. G. Millar, *The Library of A. C. Beatty: a descriptive Catalogue of the Western Manuscripts*, 4 vols. (Oxford, 1927–30), No. 9.
[2] Chester Beatty sale, Sotheby, 7 June 1932, lot 13; now in Boston Public Library.
[3] Millar No. 22.   [4] Millar No. 17.

from any purchase, it gives me the greatest pleasure to let such an enthusiast as yourself see some of the fine works that happen to be in my possession.'

On this occasion Fenwick parted with six manuscripts[1] for £2470, and later in the year a further two[2] were added for £850.

By this time a cordial friendship had grown up between the two men, and Sir Chester was able to do Fenwick several disinterested acts of kindness, foremost among them the introduction of Dr A. S. W. Rosenbach, whose massive purchases from the Phillipps Library will be recorded shortly. It was also at his suggestion that Fenwick offered one of his greatest treasures, No. 10298, a superb copy of the *Livre de la Chasse* of Gaston de Foix with eighty-seven miniatures, to Calouste Gulbenkian. That great collector was introduced to Fenwick in London by Sir Chester, but after a good deal of deliberation declined the proffered manuscript.

In March 1924 Sir Chester informed Fenwick that a catalogue of his Western manuscripts was being prepared and with this in view he would like to make another purchase, 'a more important one'. Fenwick was unwell this year and spent several months at Bath, but in July the proposed visit took place and seven manuscripts and two fragments changed hands for £5105. Four of these (Nos. 12260, 12261, 12263 and 12264) were eighth- or early ninth-century manuscripts from the well-known Italian abbey of Nonantola. Phillipps had owned a group of five manuscripts, all originally from this monastic house, bought from Payne and Foss in 1848, and the fifth (No. 12262) was already in Sir Chester's hands, having formed part of his transaction of the previous year.[3] This grasping of a rare opportunity to secure fine codices of such

[1] Four of them, Nos. 6546, 8400, 10190 and 12262, were of the eighth or ninth centuries.

[2] Nos. 389 and 390, both of the tenth century.

[3] Three of the group (Nos. 12260, 12261 and 12263) were sold when part of Sir Chester's manuscripts were auctioned by Messrs Sotheby on 7 June 1932 and 9 May 1933. Four other Nonantola MSS. (Nos. 12226, 12265, 12267 and 12268) of the tenth and eleventh centuries are in the possession of Lionel and Philip Robinson.

an early date, almost unobtainable in commerce, gave the Beatty collection a rare distinction of its own; and to the reader of Dr Eric Millar's noble catalogue it seems almost inconceivable today that such a varied galaxy of manuscripts was the fruit of less than ten years' collecting. This was in no small measure due to the friendly relationship, not always easy of attainment, which Sir Chester established with the owner of the Phillipps collection; and certainly few negotiations of which I have read the records ran so smoothly.

Some of the finest manuscripts, however, which now adorn the Chester Beatty Library in Dublin owe their presence there not to Sir Chester's own purchases but to a visit to Cheltenham by Mrs Beatty in November 1925. She shared to the full her husband's enthusiasm for manuscripts and formed the agreeable plan of secretly buying him some notable addition to his collection for a Christmas present. A race-meeting at Cheltenham provided a plausible pretext to enjoy a night's hospitality at Thirlestaine House, and on the eventful evening of 11 November Mrs Beatty bought eight manuscripts for £21,800—a substantial sum, but the purchase included two books which for forty years Fenwick had been resolute in his refusal to sell at any price at all. One was No. 1798, a late fourteenth-century Statius with twelve miniatures in grisaille by Altichiero himself or by some highly talented member of his atelier, which Dr Millar describes as 'standing in a class by itself'.[1] This was one of only two Meerman manuscripts which Fenwick had refused to sell to the Prussian Government in 1887. Mrs Beatty's other great treasure was No. 3502, a copy of Dictys Cretensis, written at Padua in the fifteenth century, with six large and forty-nine smaller miniatures of the school of Mantegna.[2] Fenwick had declined to sell this superb manuscript, formerly in the MacCarthy collection, to Sir Chester himself as recently as August 1924: and if £7000

[1] Millar No. 76.
[2] Not in Millar: No. CXVI in Comte Durrieu's list, 'Les Manuscrits à Peintures ...à Cheltenham', in *Bibliothèque de L'École des Chartes*, L (1889), p. 420.

apiece seemed a stiff price thirty years ago it would be almost impossible to assess the value of these two magnificent manuscripts in the open market today.

I closed my eyes and blessed you for selling me books I know you loved [wrote Mrs Beatty to Fenwick on her return to London on 13 November]. Needless to say on my arrival I was *bombarded* with questions—'Had I seen any books—if so which?' etc. etc. To which I replied 'I spent the whole evening with the *Book of the Chase*' (No. 10298) mentally hoping the Lord would forgive me...I know in my soul I will not be strongminded enough to keep the books until Xmas, so when they arrive I will give him one a day, reserving the *two great ones* for Xmas and birthday in February.

In 1920, the year which saw the beginning of the transactions with Sir Chester Beatty, an agreeable demonstration of American friendship for Great Britain took place. During that year a conference of British and American professors of English literature was held in London, and Carleton Brown, the eminent authority on English medieval texts, hit upon the happy notion of presenting a manuscript to the British Museum as a gift from the American delegates. On 1 July 1920 he approached Fenwick suggesting that as he himself would be leaving the country shortly J. A. Herbert, of the Department of Manuscripts at the Museum, should act as intermediary. Fenwick was unwilling to involve a third party and offered to include in the earliest possible sale at Sotheby's a suitable manuscript selected by Carleton Brown. No. 9803, a fifteenth-century collection of religious verse, was chosen, and on 9 July the American appealed to Fenwick to sell it outright, so that the presentation could be made without delay. The price of £160 was agreed between the two parties, Fenwick rushed the matter through the Court of Chancery and on 14 July the manuscript was duly handed over at the British Museum. In a covering letter Carleton Brown expressed the subscribers' wish that 'the gift, though a small matter in itself, might have its influence in strengthening the cordial bonds which unite British and American scholars'.

Fenwick's own relations with visiting scholars became noticeably warmer as the years went by. In particular he established most friendly personal relations with Professor Gunnar Tilander of the University of Stockholm, who paid several visits to Thirlestaine House to collate manuscripts relating to medieval hunting, and who has published an agreeable paper on the Phillipps Collection, containing some personal reminiscences of his stays at Cheltenham.[1]

In March 1923 Sir Chester Beatty, whom Fenwick had consulted about the sale of a block of manuscripts in the United States, proposed that he should bring down to Cheltenham 'the most important American dealer' Dr A. S. W. Rosenbach (1876–1952). 'The Doctor', as he was generally called, was indeed at this date perhaps the leading bookseller in the world, a position which he attained almost overnight by his staggering purchases at the tenth Britwell sale in March 1921.[2] The late Charles des Graz wrote a particularly perceptive account of this remarkable man in *The Book Collector*[3] soon after his death. He described him as a 'don manqué', and dwelt upon his 'professorial demeanour, earthy bonhomie and pungent zest for life'. His aim as a bookseller was to ensure that all first-class items which came on to the market were offered to him first, and this he achieved by spending very large sums in the auction-room with apparent lordly indifference and with the maximum of publicity. These methods did not endear him to his trade rivals, whose envy and malice were not decreased by the fact that the Doctor, by some inimitable alchemy of his own, contrived almost invariably to feature in his numerous appearances in the British press not as a bookseller but as 'the great American collector'. For some, especially in the trade, this flamboyant streak obscured his real merits, chief among them the creation of many very rich collectors and the guidance of their enthusiasms into sound and scholarly channels; nor should

[1] 'Världens största privata handschriftssamling', in *Nordisk Tidskrift för Bok- och Biblioteksväsen*, XXXIX (1952), pp. 81–92.
[2] He secured 207 out of 321 lots, and spent £40,584 of a total of £48,552.
[3] Vol. I, no. 3, Autumn 1952, pp. 177–9.

we fail to remember the disinterested help and advice which he frequently gave to young bookmen.

The first-fruit of Rosenbach's meeting with Fenwick was the purchase for £3500 of the very important military correspondence of the Marquis de Montcalm during the war in Canada in 1756–8 (3714).[1] Three printed items were secured at the same time, an indulgence on vellum printed by Gutenberg in 1455 for £2500,[2] a copy of the 1460 *Catholicon* also for £2500 and a rare *Americanum*, Bradford's *Laws and Acts of the General Assembly for Their Majesties Province of New York*, 1693–4.[3]

This transaction took place in April 1923 and two months later the Doctor's senior partner, his brother Philip, met Fenwick at the Carysfort sale and subsequently visited Cheltenham where he secured an offer from Fenwick of the whole of the incunabula which still remained in the Phillipps Library. These numbered seven hundred and seventy-four, and Fenwick's price was £20,250. On 19 July the Doctor cabled his acceptance of this figure and the greatest part of this very substantial block of fifteenth-century books passed in due course into the ownership of Henry E. Huntington. 'It may interest you to know', wrote Dr Rosenbach to Huntington on 13 July 1923, 'that I am the only bookseller that has ever inspected the [Phillipps] collection. I stayed at Cheltenham as Mr Fenwick's guest for three days when I carefully examined the collection. The only other American who ever had access to it was Mr J. P. Morgan, who purchased five illuminated manuscripts from it some years ago.' On 3 August Philip Rosenbach inquired the price of the Battle Abbey muniments, which his brother had previously inspected, and also of a group of medieval English manuscripts, both poetry and prose. On the former (Nos. 9887–9940) Fenwick set the figure of £3750, which was accepted by Rosenbach on Huntington's

[1] Sold to the National Archives of Canada for $27,600.
[2] Sold to Morgan for $25,000.
[3] Now in the Rosenbach Foundation, Philadelphia. From the binding of this copy Wilberforce Eames extracted unique fragments of the earliest New York printing; these are now in the New York Public Library.

behalf. Twenty English manuscripts were selected, including four of Chaucer, two of Langland and one astrological manuscript which had belonged to John Dee. Fenwick's price of £11,870 was thought to be on the high side and on 28 September Rosenbach cabled from Philadelphia.

In regard to 20 English MSS our client [Huntington] offers us reduction and if you can accept £11,000 subject court approval we can close deal at small profit to ourselves. Thought it could go through at same time as Battle Abbey please cable reply immediately advise acceptance as client is not well and leaving next Tuesday for California.

Fenwick was in Italy and only after some delay did he cable a counter-proposal of £11,500, a price which Rosenbach accepted by return. Seventeen of the twenty manuscripts passed into the Henry E. Huntington Library for $92,000, which in a single transaction acquired a respectable holding of a class of text which has become progressively rare in commerce.

If in these transactions Rosenbach paid full current market prices, or even sums in excess of them, he contrived to secure in his next purchase what was, in my estimation, a considerable bargain. In May 1924 he paid £4960 for twelve items. One was a printed book of which I have no proper record; of the other eleven nine were manuscript atlases and portulans of the sixteenth or seventeenth centuries, including No. 13199, Nicolas Vallard's splendidly illuminated atlas of the world, with pictorial drawings, executed in 1547.[1] The two remaining manuscripts comprised No. 8558, a large collection of early papers relating to the American colonies, bound in ten volumes,[2] and No. 3504, the fine early twelfth-century Bible associated with the name of Gundulf, Bishop of Rochester.[3] So far as I can compute this group of manuscripts had cost Phillipps between five and six hundred pounds, and doubtless to Fenwick an almost tenfold appreciation must have seemed a sufficiently handsome advance on the cost

[1] Huntington MS. HM. 29.
[2] Sold to Huntington for $30,000.
[3] Huntington MS. HM. 62.

price: nevertheless the Gundulf Bible alone would today be worth many times the sum which was paid for the whole group, and the portulans have likewise since 1924 been powerfully affected by the rise in prices which has been especially conspicuous in the field of early scientific books.

At the meeting when this group of manuscripts changed hands Rosenbach inquired about the Spanish manuscripts in the collection, and Fenwick undertook to prepare a list. This proved unexpectedly onerous, for there turned out to be between twelve and thirteen hundred of them, and Fenwick toiled for three months at the task. He eventually set a price of £13,965 on the collection. Six years later they were still unsold, although in 1928 Rosenbach had hopes that 'a university in the West' would acquire them. In 1924 he pressed Fenwick to compile also a catalogue of all his remaining early English manuscripts with a view to selling them to Huntington. Fenwick made a start but was handicapped, first by eye trouble and indifferent health, and later by the serious illness of his brother, which necessitated a prolonged visit to Switzerland. Details of a transaction in May 1925 are not available, but in that month Rosenbach paid Fenwick £5600, which probably represents the purchase of a further batch of early English texts. In March 1926 Rosenbach set off for England: his two sisters died while he was *en route* and in sending his condolences Fenwick added a warm invitation to visit Cheltenham. On this occasion Rosenbach bought for £7800 three editions of Columbus letters and four of Vespucci voyages,[1] together with a manuscript *Bible Hystoriale* and a copy of the Gospels of which I have no particulars.

In May 1928 Rosenbach bought for £10,000 the magnificent manuscript of Gaston de Foix's *Livre de la Chasse* (No. 10298), which Gulbenkian had declined four years earlier.[2] The last purchase of which I find any record was in May 1930, when the

[1] Sold for $63,000 to Herschel V. Jones.
[2] Declined by Morgan in 1928 for $165,000 and subsequently sold to Miss Clara Peck of Lexington, Kentucky, U.S.A.

American dealer paid £4000 for two editions of Eliot's Indian *Bible*, an early engraving[1] and two albums of Old Master drawings by Giulio Romano and Federico Zuccaro.[2]

Rosenbach was the only bookseller who secured the coveted entrée to Thirlestaine House, for on the whole Fenwick shared his grandfather's distrust of the trade and rebuffed several offers from dealers who wished to act as his agent or who had been instructed to approach him by their customers. Since, in a sense, Fenwick was the greatest bookseller of them all, with an inexhaustible stock of fabulous richness to draw upon, this somewhat disdainful attitude evoked a good deal of resentment. 'His craftiness is only excelled by his greediness', wrote one disgruntled dealer tartly to Morgan's Librarian. Rosenbach however, no ordinary bookseller admittedly, found him a straightforward and easy person with whom to conduct business. In the transactions of which I have examined the records (and there may well be others) he laid out over £70,000, a figure larger than that expended on Phillipps books by any other individual or institution in Fenwick's lifetime.[3]

Some of the transactions previously chronicled may have given an impression of Fenwick as an uncompromising driver of hard bargains, unwilling from any considerations of reason or sentiment to budge from the position which he had adopted at the outset of a negotiation. As age mellowed him, however, this trait was progressively modified, and in the last private sale in which he was engaged it is pleasant to record an agreement reached with the greatest goodwill and friendliness on both sides. No small share of this happy conclusion was due to the charm and tact of the Irish Government's representative, Dr Richard Irvine Best (d. 1959,

---

[1] 'Head and Bust of a Man in a Fantastic Helmet' (Hind A.I. 56), formerly attributed to Verrocchio, sold to Mr Lessing J. Rosenwald in 1938 for $4850.

[2] Both in the Rosenbach Foundation, Philadelphia. The Romano group has been reattributed to Girolamo da Carpi.

[3] I am very greatly indebted to Mr Edwin Wolf 2nd, Librarian of the Library Company of Philadelphia, for making valuable additions and corrections to my draft account of the Rosenbach transactions. Mr Wolf's biography of 'The Doctor' is eagerly awaited.

aged 87), Director of the National Library of Ireland from 1924 to 1940 and Chairman of the Irish Manuscripts Commission.

On 8 March 1929 Dr Best wrote to ask whether he could come to Cheltenham to examine Irish manuscripts in the Phillipps Collection, not only to take notes on behalf of the Irish Manuscripts Commission but also with a view to the purchase of some of them, if any were for sale. The visit took place in November 1930. Dr Best has been kind enough to send me extracts from several letters which he wrote to his wife during his stay at Thirlestaine House.

Mr Fenwick received me on arrival in the drawing-room in the friendliest manner [he wrote], and afterwards his sister, Mrs Fielden, who was staying with him. Robin Flower[1] had not arrived, nor did he until the dinner bell sounded. I chatted with Mr Fenwick in the meanwhile, and at about 7.30 he brought me up to the bedroom assigned to me. Thirlestaine House is a splendid mansion, with spacious rooms opening on to one another, somewhat like our Vice-Regal Lodge. The walls are hung with family and other portraits, and the drawing-room with large 18th-century landscapes. My bedroom is a beautiful spacious room, furnished almost like a drawing-room, sofas, couches, armchairs, occasional tables, etc., etc., a warm fire in the grate. . . . It is a beautiful house, the stairs and passages all in white, doors same, with carved borders. We had a sumptuous dinner. Mr Fenwick reminds me of George Moore's brother, the Colonel, the same nice manner, so friendly. Mrs Fielden too is quite charming. She remembers her grandfather Sir Thomas Phillipps and the removal from their old home, Middlehill to Cheltenham. She says most of the great manuscripts are still in the library, with thousands of others. I wonder. Their great dread is fire. One did occur some years ago, but fortunately no damage was done to the library. Mr Fenwick rolls back the rugs from before the fire at night, so that no sparks or live coals may alight on them. . . .

From my window I see the massive columns of the mansion. There is a public road in front with cars passing. That is the drawback, as Mr Fenwick remarked 'The town has obtruded on the house'. There are clocks everywhere which strike gently. In fact silence reigns over this splendid abode. One walks over Persian carpets laid on parquet

[1] Robin Ernest William Flower (d. 1946), Deputy Keeper of MSS., British Museum, 1929–44.

floors and up broad stone stairs and down long corridors in which no footfall is heard; they are lined with Queen Anne chairs and family portraits hung on the walls. One never encounters a servant, only the jaded old valet who told me that when a boy he was page to Archbishop Beresford of Armagh.

After breakfast Flower and I got to work. Mr Fenwick and the valet kept bringing armfuls of Mss. into the drawing-room for us to examine. There seemed no end to them. Before lunch we both felt exhausted. All the drawing-room windows were closed. So we went into the grounds for a while. Mr Fenwick was there too. But we could not stay long, for it was very cold. After lunch we fell to again and worked until 5 o'c tea. Then we walked into town....

Next day at 8.45 a.m. Flower and I went down to tackle the Mss. again. I thought I was getting the 'flu, I felt so done up, but after lunch and some air it passed off. I am not sure whether I shall be able to come to terms with Mr Fenwick. On seeing that we were separating the sheep from the goats, he began to have doubts as to whether he would part with the Mss. After dinner I pointed out to him what were several copies in Ms. of a printed book, and we after a while came on the rare book itself,[1] of which there is only one copy in Ireland—in the Franciscan Convent. He is fully alive to all this, but makes no suggestion. I have talked it all over with Flower. I'm afraid Mr Fenwick may turn out difficult to deal with. He isn't obliged to sell anything, and can therefore bide his time. Possibly he has an exaggerated notion of their value in the market. Yet I feel we should acquire all the vellums. We remained in the drawing-room looking over those he had assembled after tea, until it was 11 p.m. and Mrs Fielden had retired. It seemed rude to neglect her so but we had no alternative. In the afternoon Mr Fenwick for the first time brought us into the Ms. Store, and showed us some of the greater treasures. They were extremely beautiful, one of them an illuminated Giraldus Cambrensis. Flower was much impressed. There must be at least ten thousand Mss. still there, out of the original sixty or a hundred thousand. They are in the boxes in which they were transferred from Middlehill in 1862. These boxes stand one on top of another up to the ceiling like patent shelves, the lids having been cut off, all save the tops, the chains hanging down with the padlocks attached, so that one can't remove many of the volumes. I could have stayed another night with profit, but Flower had to go.

[1] Michael O'Clery, *Foclóir nó-sanasán Nua*, Louvain, 1643.

He was excellent company at dinner, telling many stories of the Blasket islanders. He drove off with a friend to Gloucester. This afternoon I had a look at the Picture Gallery of the mansion, full of 'old masters', most of them spoiled, in my opinion, by cleaners, also at a collection of Glover's huge landscapes, dull things with scarcely a sparkle of light or colour, no doubt the acquisitions of Sir Thomas Phillipps, who had much better taste in Mss.

Dr Best had previously examined the brief and imperfect account of the Irish manuscripts published by H. d'Arbois de Jubainville,[1] and their true extent and quality were a surprise to him. Phillipps had bought very actively at the dispersals of the libraries of many Irish antiquaries and collectors, such as Austin Cooper, Edward O'Reilly, Shaw and Monck Mason, Sir William Betham and J. H. Todd, and had also commissioned many transcripts of Irish material on his own account: and the final total of manuscripts which Dr Best noted as desirable acquisitions by the Irish Government amounted to one hundred and seventy-eight volumes. It was not until 29 January 1931 that Fenwick found time to set his valuation on them, and the figure, £2750, was considerably in excess of the would-be purchaser's estimate of their worth.

Your letter conveys the impression [wrote Dr Best on 7 February 1931] that it has not been without a struggle that you have taken the decision to sell, and that the sum you mention is in a sense the measure of your reluctance to part with the manuscripts. I felt this from the outset, and was prepared for a high estimate on your part, but I did not anticipate anything like so high a figure as £2750, which appears to me to be based on an erroneous conception of their value. In this matter, if I may say so, I have experience of over twenty-five years both as editor and keeper of Irish Mss., and have purchased them in the sale rooms. In the circumstances I would not feel justified in recommending their acquisition at the price named. Sentiment no doubt plays a not inconsiderable part with you, and I must admit it does to a certain extent with us also. Can we not meet on this basis? To recover the Mss. for their home of origin we are prepared to make some sacrifice

---

[1] *Essai d'un Catalogue de la Littérature épique de l'Irlande* (Paris, 1883), pp. xcvi–xcvii.

6-2

and pay perhaps even more than the actual state of the market would appear to justify. Your Trustees on the other hand might be led to view with satisfaction the permanent preservation of the collection in the National Library of Ireland, where it would continue to be known to future generations as the 'Phillipps Collection'.

In putting the matter up to the Department of Finance, my Trustees will naturally have to be guided by expert advice, and here I may remark that Dr Flower, who is the leading authority on Irish Mss., has mentioned £1,000 as a generous price to pay for the collection. His report on the importance of the manuscripts will carry great weight.

Meantime I earnestly beg you to reconsider your estimate, for I should regret it more than I could possibly say if negotiations were to break down for want of a right understanding.

In a courteous reply of 9 February Fenwick conceded that his estimate might be too high, but felt that the gap between the two figures was so large as to be almost unbridgeable. It was, he pointed out, doubtless on the value of the most important items that their estimates were at variance, and on these he thought that comparatively little could be conceded. Dr Best replied by return of post expressing his disappointment.

My Trustees do not meet until Friday [he added], that is the day after tomorrow, when I shall lay your letter before them. Meantime I am reluctant to consider the matter as closed, and in view of what I intimated in my letter, that the Trustees, in order to recover the Mss., would be likely to make a sacrifice and pay more than what would appear to be the market value, might I ask you to let me know what is the irreducible minimum which you would ask your Trustees to sanction. The matter is urgent as the Trustees must at this meeting apply for any special grant that they may need in the coming financial year.

Fenwick's prices were not arrived at capriciously or without much research. He invariably ascertained from bills and catalogues the original cost to Phillipps of as many items as he could trace. On most of these figures he of course made a substantial advance, but on by no means all, for he was fully alive to the changes in taste which had caused certain classes of manuscripts to decline in value over the previous century. His detailed calculations in this transaction are preserved among his papers. He worked over the list afresh and on 12 February wrote offering what was for him an unprecedented reduction. The new figure was £1850, a price which on 14 February the Trustees of the National Library of Ireland accepted with 'an expression of their high appreciation of the friendly and sympathetic manner in which Fenwick had met their wishes'.

After the customary formalities in the Court of Chancery the manuscripts were collected by Dr Best in person on 3 March.

It was with something of the collector's thrill, if not his sense of ownership [wrote Dr Best from the National Library on 6 March], that I spread the precious vellums out on my writing table at home, preparatory to bringing them in here. Now the whole collection is safely deposited in the Ms. strong room, their final home I hope. The Minister of Finance is coming to see them on Tuesday, and when I shall have time to make a proper Hand List of their contents I shall be expected to give a private exhibition of them to the high officers of State and Departmental Heads.

It has all been most exciting. The transfer has taken place with such rapidity that I myself hardly yet realise it. But the pleasant days that I passed under your hospitable roof will remain abiding memories.

The acquisition was the more important to the young Republic because of the catastrophe which Irish historical studies had suffered nine years before when the Dublin Public Record Office and its contents perished in the burning of the Four Courts during the Troubles. While nothing could repair that loss the Phillipps accession was no mean consolation. Fourteen of the hundred and seventy-eight manuscripts[1] were on vellum, and included a detached portion (8214) of the Yellow Book of Lecan in the Library of Trinity College, Dublin, a fine medical manuscript (10297) containing the only extant version of the ancient law

---

[1] Listed by Dr Best in an appendix to his *Report to the Council of Trustees of the National Library of Ireland*, 1931, pp. 15–27. The list was reprinted, together with a description of the Phillipps manuscripts purchased at Sotheby's on 27–8 June, 1938, in the *Report* of 1939.

tracts *Bretha Crólige* and *Bretha Déin Checht*, the life of *Féchín of Fore* (9194) and the *Félire of Oengus* (17082).

Throughout the transaction one gets an agreeable impression of Fenwick's reasonableness, induced, we may be sure, by his personal liking for the Irish negotiator, whose infectious enthusiasm for his role permeates all his letters. Future generations of Irish scholars will have good reason to be grateful to Dr Best, who secured for his nation the last collection of early Irish manuscripts still in private hands; nor should they forget the share of Mr Ernest Blythe, the enlightened Minister of Finance, who provided the funds.

The sales by auction held between 1919 and 1938 cannot rival their pre-Great War counterparts, and apart from the first of them, which began on 24 June 1919, they were of comparatively little moment. During the third decade of the century Fenwick was fully occupied with the substantial private sales chronicled above, and he was far too astute a man of business to put many books of major importance into the sales of the 'thirties, when prices had dropped to such a degree that they could tempt only an owner who was compelled to sell.

The remaining sales at Sotheby's which took place in Fenwick's lifetime may be tabulated thus:

xvii.	24–7 June 1919	939 lots	MSS.	£9207. 2s. 6d.
xviii.	9–10 July 1928	414 lots	printed books	£3770. 14s. 0d.
xix.	17–18 June 1935	436 lots	printed books	£1893. 16s. 0d.
xx.	24–5 June 1935	507 lots	MSS.	£5318. 18s. 0d.
xxi.	29–30 June 1936	512 lots	MSS.	£2194. 15s. 0d.
xxii.	27–8 June 1938	513 lots	MSS.	£3401. 8s. 0d.
		3321		£25,786. 13s. 6d.

The seventeenth sale included a few printed books, and Fenwick with a shrewd eye to the market inserted no less than 550 lots of *Americana*. The most important of these sold, by the standard of the day, very well. On behalf of the New York Public Library Quaritch paid £470 for a wood-engraving illustrating South

American Indians executed in Germany about 1505 (xvii, 57),[1] and the same firm gave £255 for lot 155, Michael Lok's account of Martin Frobisher's third voyage for the discovery of the North-West Passage in 1578 (20821)[2] and £345 for lot 522, three volumes of the journal of the Council for the Plantations, covering the period 1672–86 (8539). Other *Americana* included a large amount of material relating to Mexico, much of it from the Kingsborough papers, and many printed books in the Indian dialects. Sir William Osler bought several groups of historical papers relating to Canada (xvii, 110–113). A few lots must be accounted bargains even by the less inflated prices of forty years ago, and in this context one may cite lot 99, Cuthbert Pudsey's contemporary account of his residence in Brazil from 1629 to 1640 (13312), which seems to have been undervalued at £9, and lot 152 at £72, Benjamin Franklin's autograph draft of notes for intending immigrants to America (26198). Fenwick bought in for £140 and £165 lots 528 and 529, two portulans (23856 and 16365) which later passed to Henry E. Huntington through Dr Rosenbach, but he let two fifteenth-century manuscripts on vellum of Dante go for £29 and £16 respectively (18797: xvii, 657 and 23255: xvii, 658). The highest price in the sale was £710, paid by Sotheran for lot 880, a volume of eight Shakespeare quartos which Fenwick had bought in at the sale of 1897 for £170 (ix, 691); this figure was almost equalled by another lot of Shakespearean interest, a collection of original letters of Sir John Fastolf (9735: xvii, 671) for which Quaritch gave £690 on behalf of the British Museum.[3] The same bookseller paid £260 for another notable item, the original manuscript of King James's *Daemonologie* (2713: xvii, 787).[4]

The printed books sold on 9 and 10 July 1928 were of no great interest. Many were imperfect, and Fenwick at this sale dis-

---

[1] Described with an account of the previous history of the woodcut by Wilberforce Eames in *The Bulletin of the New York Public Library*, September 1922. I am indebted to Mr Karl Kup for this information.
[2] Huntington MS. 715.　　　　　[3] B.M. Add. MSS. 39848 and 39849.
[4] Folger Shakespeare Library 1125. 1.

encumbered his shelves of some lengthy runs of periodicals. He included however a number of first editions of eighteenth-century English literature, then at the peak of its popularity, and Messrs Pickering and Chatto paid £215 for a copy of *The Vanity of Human Wishes* (xviii, 192), a figure which it is interesting to compare with the £150 which the same firm gave for the Rawlinson–Bright presentation copy of Drayton's *The Muses Elizium*, 1630 (xviii, 115). It was not until June 1935 that Fenwick tested the market after the spectacular fall of values in the slump of five years before. Prices for the printed books sold on 17 and 18 June were very modest: two collections of Statutes and Year Books printed by Pynson (xix, 349 and 433) fetched £105 apiece, and a respectable copy of the *editio princeps* of Aristophanes (xix, 13) £58. A considerable bargain was an imperfect copy of the romance of Jean d'Arras, *La Melusine* (xix, 174). Properly described as an unrecorded fifteenth-century edition in contemporary stamped calf by Caxton's second binder, this fine book with full-page woodcuts realized only £32.[1] In the sale of manuscripts on the 24th and 25th of the same month there was a sprinkling of more valuable items. Maggs Brothers paid £235 for Peter Briscoe's journal of his voyage to the South Seas in Captain Cook's *Endeavour* (17111: xx, 78), P. J. Dobell £86 for a volume of Matthew Prior's diplomatic correspondence (8677: xx, 353) and Messrs Quaritch £120 for the documents relating to the two trials of John Wilkes for the publication of No. 45 of the *North Briton* and the *Essay on Woman* (15109–11: xx, 484). In selling the last lot Messrs Sotheby established an interesting precedent by sealing up the manuscripts of the *Essay on Woman* and *The Universal Prayer* and allowing no prospective buyer to view them, thus avoiding infringement of the law which bans the display for sale of obscene literature. A fine tenth-century volume of tracts

[1] It recently passed into the collection of Major J. R. Abbey: subsequent research has confirmed that no other copy is recorded of this edition, printed at Lyons by Martin Huss for B. Buyer between 1478 and 1484. It had previously belonged to Heber. See Mr Arthur Rau's note in *Bibliothèque d'Humanisme et Renaissance*, XVII (1956), pp. 429–31.

by Boniface and others, with interesting initials, was bought by Seymour de Ricci for £165 (8462: xx, 40), a low figure, as was the mere £52 which lot 152 realized, the twelfth-century Caerleon–Hayles manuscript of Gregory's *Homilies* (12357: xx, 152), which Dr Eric Millar has recently transferred from his own collection to the British Museum.[1] Several monastic cartularies fetched between £66 and £180, some of the most interesting being bought by Mr H. R. Creswick for Cambridge University Library,[2] along with other shrewd purchases. Those of us who saw Sir Sydney Cockerell's Renaissance manuscripts sold in 1957 for large sums will recall with a pang that in 1935 Mr Creswick was able to buy for £18 a fifteenth-century text of Martial written on vellum and signed by the scribe.[3] A whole group of seventeenth-century English poetical miscellanies sold for sums ranging between £10. 10s. 0d. and £28.

One item, however, in the sale of 1935 stands out in providing a romantic example of the sort of discovery which can still be made by an assiduous and discriminating collector with good luck on his side. Lot 144 bore a modest description in the catalogue, 'A Geographical Commonplace book or dictionary of the Holy Land Asia Minor and Syria, with various maps neatly drawn and coloured, about the year 1600...'.[4] Its subject-matter appealed to Mr Walter Oakeshott, then a master at Winchester, now Rector of Lincoln College, Oxford. He took advice from a leading London bookseller, who informed him that if any other collector were interested it might sell for as much as £40, but that it might well fetch a comparatively modest sum. The latter view proved to be correct and Mr Oakeshott bought the manuscript for £4. 5s. 0d.

He found himself to be the owner of a commonplace book in vellum covers, the leaves lettered alphabetically to form a sort of geographical glossary of the Middle East, illustrated with a dozen manuscript maps, and containing also an early library list and a

[1] Add. MS. 48984.
[2] E.g. 23628: xx, 50: U.L.C. Add. 6847; and 6960: xx, 63: U.L.C. Add. 6845.
[3] 16344: xx, 292: U.L.C. Add. 6849.
[4] 6339, formerly in Lord Guilford's Library and acquired by Phillipps in 1830.

poem of seven four-line stanzas. 'It was always a satisfactory possession,' Mr Oakeshott wrote to me on 1 November 1957, 'for it had those maps and the library lists of someone whose interests were similar to some of my own; with the travel books, science, medicine, etc.' It remained on his shelves for seventeen years during which, other interests and the war supervening, he did not make it the object of any sustained research.

In 1952 he decided to sell a group of books and he took them, the manuscript included, to a London dealer. From that moment fortune smiled upon him. In the first place none of the principals of the firm was available and so the deal could not be clinched upon the spot. He left the books and went on to the British Museum, where an exhibition had been mounted to commemorate the fourth centenary of the births of Hakluyt and Raleigh.

As soon as I saw the Raleigh material *in extenso* [Mr Oakeshott recounts] I saw at once the similarity of the various hands to those of the notebook. When I got back I wrote to the bookseller to say that the Ms. was not for sale. It was very clear that if it *was* Raleigh, it must link up with the *History of the World*, so I compared the two and found, especially over Egypt, striking similarities of phrasing. It was indeed beyond doubt that there was *some* connexion between the two.

At this stage he enlisted the aid of the Department of Manuscripts of the British Museum, and having there outlined his views on the notebook received from the Keeper 'the kind of look that heads of the Ms. Department give to well-known Baconians'. Detailed examination of the text by Mr T. C. Skeat however revealed two points which established beyond any shadow of doubt that the manuscript was Raleigh's own commonplace book, written in the Tower during the long years of his imprisonment and containing notes made in preparation for his *History*. Mr Oakeshott wrote an account of the discovery in *The Times* of 29 November 1952, and this important Phillipps manuscript passed, very suitably, into the possession of Messrs Lionel and Philip Robinson, who cheerfully paid £3000 to secure this evocative memorial of one of the greatest Elizabethans.

The sales of 1936 and 1938 need not detain us long. Both contained many lots of English deeds, which sold for very modest prices; one may instance xxi, 512, one hundred and forty-four court-rolls on vellum of the manor of Elmley Castle, Worcestershire. This fine series, extending from 20 Edward III to 25 Elizabeth, fetched £21 or about three shillings a roll. In the final sale Maggs Brothers secured for £165 the manuscript autobiography of 'General' Joseph Holt (1756–1826), the Irish rebel of 1798 who was sent as a convict to Australia (13235: xxii, 278). There was a substantial block of material relating to Ireland in the sale (xxii, 221–308), the most important of which Dr Best was successful in securing for the National Library. This included the original charter of Prince John, *Dominus Hiberniæ*, confirming the grant of the city of Dublin by his father Henry II to the people of Bristol (33747: xxii, 288); this precious document, drawn up at Kildare in 1185, was certainly not overvalued at £110.

We have noted in youth and middle age a tendency in Fenwick to drive a hard bargain, an unaccommodating strain which may have sprung less from the Phillipps blood in his veins than from his somewhat anomalous position. Even today, when the turning into cash of ancestral possessions is a commonplace, not all gentlemen contrive to carry out the task with grace and charm. 'No good ever came of gentlemen buying and selling', wrote John Hill Burton, and before 1914 society at large would have endorsed this view. It was, I think, this frame of mind which led Fenwick to insist rather too loudly on his amateur status and on the private nature of the library, though one must not underrate the difficulty of keeping would-be purchasers at bay and thus preserving the right to sell the books in his own manner and his own time. To the judgement of a manuscript's value he applied a highly professional eye, although the envy of the trade sometimes asserted otherwise. The late Charles des Graz used to praise his expert knowledge of prices, and his step-daughter has told me how she travelled up to one of the sales at Sotheby's with him, and how Fenwick on the journey marked his catalogue with the estimated value of each lot and, having added up the totals on the return journey, discovered that his estimate was within a hundred pounds of the sum actually realized.

If, however, one were not negotiating for a block of manuscripts Fenwick was a man of considerable personal charm, an excellent host and a genial figure at many racecourses, for he had a lifelong love of the Turf. In 1936 he married a second time, and once more a widow, Mrs Every-Halsted, an old family friend who had often acted as his hostess. To his second wife's daughter, Mrs Haywood, I owe a few details of life at Thirlestaine House. The library wing was extremely gloomy, for the shutters were rarely opened and the windows never. All the rooms were full of the rough box shelves built into bays with tall cases back to back in the middle of a central corridor. Over the library presided Edwin Rogers, who died in 1934 after sixty-nine years of continuous service with the family. Skull-capped and bearded, his ritual entry bearing the morning's post made a deep impression on a visitor. The indoor domestic staff of the great house was small, a butler, a cook and a daily housemaid; and the butler, who had mastered the rudiments of court-hand, spent his leisure sorting vellum deeds into the counties to which they related. The kitchens, as in Phillipps's day, remained separated from the house by a lane, and the food was wheeled through a tunnel on a trolley. Nevertheless visitors to Thirlestaine House have lively memories of the comfort of their stay there, and of the attentive kindliness of their host.

This kindliness, so Mrs Haywood told me, was shown particularly to children and young people; and of this I have first-hand evidence. It is now rather more than a quarter of a century since the writer of these *Phillipps Studies*, then, I think, a first-year undergraduate, diffidently pulled the bell at a gate in the high wall which at that time surrounded Thirlestaine House. As I approached the front door its owner was waiting to greet me. The visit had been arranged by my father, who had met Fenwick at the house of a mutual friend, and having told him of my precocious interest in old books had received an invitation for me to take tea with him.

THOMAS FITZROY FENWICK

He led me through the long galleries of pictures with impressive names on their frames, and I was duly awed by a large room hung entirely with landscapes by John Glover, an artist of whom I had never heard. The Catlin gallery was admired in turn and we then had tea, at the end of which, unable to disguise my impatience any longer, I asked if I might see the library. Fenwick shook his head regretfully. The library, he said, was not shown to visitors. Then, seeing my obvious disappointment, he smiled and said that some of the best books would be brought to us in the drawing-room. He rang the bell and the butler carried in two trays laden with manuscripts, perhaps two dozen of them, ranging in date from the ninth to the sixteenth century. One by one Fenwick opened them and discoursed upon their script and decoration. He had the rare gift of being able to instruct the young without patronage and to make them feel that they had something worth-while to contribute to the discussion. Two hours sped by before he had finished, in the course of which I had handled the finest group of medieval manuscripts in private hands at that date. I left in a kind of trance, bemused by the splendour of it all, and I have often since recollected the charm and disinterested kindness of Thomas FitzRoy Fenwick in sacrificing an afternoon to give inexpressible pleasure to an ignorant youth who was a complete stranger to him.

1938–1957

Thomas FitzRoy Fenwick died at the age of eighty-two on 1 September 1938. During his life-tenancy, and that of his mother before him, the proceeds of the many sales had been invested as capital trust funds. At his death these considerable funds, Thirlestaine House, the pictures and the residue of the great library passed to his nephew, Alan George Fenwick, elder son of the late Lt.-Col. M. J. E. Fenwick. Mr Alan Fenwick was tenant for life under a Deed of Resettlement of the trust property, which after negotiations between him and his uncle he had executed before the latter's death. He continued to farm his estate at Wendover, Buckinghamshire, and a large share of the burden of maintaining Thirlestaine House under adverse conditions and the onerous responsibility for the future of the Library fell on the shoulders of his wife. Fate decreed that their enjoyment of Thirlestaine House and its very valuable contents was unhappily short-lived. At the outbreak of war in September 1939 Government departments turned covetous eyes on the spacious galleries of the mansion at Cheltenham, and it was duly requisitioned by the Ministry of Aircraft Production. The Ministry urgently called for the library wing to be cleared with all speed, and the great collection, with all the literature and records relating to it, was hastily crated up and stored in the cellars for the duration. Perhaps it was as well

94

that Thomas FitzRoy Fenwick did not live to witness this up-heaval, which would certainly have caused him deep distress. It is striking to think that a year after his death the whole contents of the Manuscript Room and the Great Room where the remainder of the library was kept were removed to the cellars, never again to return to the place which Sir Thomas Phillipps had provided for their preservation and in which Thomas FitzRoy Fenwick had spent his adult life in study and investigation of them.

The estate at his death became liable for death duty at a high rate on the trust property, although exemption was granted in respect of the whole of the manuscripts, unless and until they were sold. It was apparent both to the life-tenant and to his Trustees that the future marketing of sections of the Phillipps Collection would be fraught with peculiar difficulties. For more than half a century Thomas FitzRoy Fenwick had devoted his great abilities, his time and his expert knowledge of manuscripts to the problem of the library's orderly dispersal, and he had in effect kept all negotiations in his own capable hands. It would have been unreasonable to expect in yet another generation of the family the combination of palaeographical skill and astute knowledge of the book-market which had characterized Sir Thomas's nephew. Nevertheless it was in the interest of the life-tenant that the sales should continue and that thus the income from the trust funds should be periodically increased as it had been throughout his uncle's life, particularly as very heavy inroads had been made upon them for death duty. Moreover by 1944 it was becoming clear that Thirlestaine House would probably not be suitable as a private residence in the post-war period, and that the re-establishment of the great library and the responsibility for making its contents available to the learned world would present a variety of grave problems. The time therefore might be approaching when it would be a logical and sensible step to sell the vast residue of the collection *en bloc*.

Some exploratory moves were made in this direction in 1944,

and when Lionel Robinson, senior partner of William H. Robinson Limited, visited New York in the course of that year he found that photographs of certain Phillipps manuscripts were in circulation and that a syndicate was being formed to conduct negotiations. On his return to London he discussed the matter with his partner and brother Philip, and together they decided that the most strenuous efforts should be made to secure the prize for the firm of Robinson.

Before recounting the negotiations through which this ambition was realized it is worth digressing to trace the history and development of this remarkable business, founded in 1881 by William Horsley Robinson at Newcastle upon Tyne, where the parent firm still exists. Developed by the founder's son Lionel Edward Robinson (father of the present Lionel and Philip) and by William Horsley, Junior (their uncle), it differed in no way from scores of other provincial bookshops. Newcastle is a centre of wide cultural activities and has always supported several good booksellers, among which the Robinson shop, with its modest stock of new and second-hand books, has long been numbered.

It was not until 1918, when the present Lionel Robinson was demobilized after distinguished service in the First World War, that the firm began to assume a new character. Lionel, then aged twenty-one, spent a few months with the well-known London house of Henry Sotheran before returning to Newcastle, and in 1919, in conjunction with his brother Philip, he opened a rare-book department in the family business.

At a very early date the young partners learned the lesson that country auction-sales were, as a source of acquiring stock, distasteful, time-consuming and unprofitable. The activities of the 'Ring' have recently been much in the public eye and in those unreformed days the presence at any major country sale of a powerful combination of booksellers from London made it almost impossible for a provincial dealer to secure any of the important lots. From this early distaste of the 'settlement' grew up a characteristic which has been perhaps the most striking feature of the house of Robinson, the purchase of an over-whelmingly large proportion of its stock by private treaty outside the auction-room. The buying of libraries privately is of course an aim common to all antiquarian booksellers, but probably no other firm during the present century has devoted such persistence, skill and research to this particular end, and certainly no other firm has achieved such spectacularly successful results. Initially the brothers sought to make arrangements with auctioneers by which they bought libraries *en bloc* before a sale, and their first success by this method was the acquisition of the library at Stanwick Hall, Yorkshire. Soon however they actively sought out owners of books on their own, and by paying prices generous by comparison with those of their trade rivals they soon became known among the country gentlemen of the North of England as a local firm which might with confidence be consulted about the disposal of an ancestral library. These early years were marked by a number of substantial private purchases, and by 1924 the Robinsons were able to mount an exhibition at King's College (then Armstrong College), Newcastle, containing among other items a dozen medieval manuscripts and a similar number of important in-cunabula. The same year saw the purchase of the residue of the library at Newburgh Priory, Yorkshire,[1] where the books were in exceptionally fine condition, a factor to which the firm paid increasing attention.

During the nineteen-twenties the political situation in Ireland made it a particularly fruitful hunting-ground. Many great houses were likely to become the target of incendiaries, and their owners sought to forestall the holocaust by turning into cash their pictures, plate and libraries. In this troubled period the brothers Robinson travelled the country extensively and their enterprise was rewarded by many discoveries. Among important purchases may be singled out the library of Dr Johnson's Blue-stocking friend Mrs Vesey. Bought in 1926 from Lucan House, Co. Dublin, this valuable collection was the subject of a special catalogue

[1] Described in Catalogue No. 12.

(No. 14). By 1929 the two brothers in their modest upstairs premises were widely known in the antiquarian book-world and enjoyed the confidence of collectors of the calibre of Sir Leicester Harmsworth, who entrusted a substantial number of his duplicates to them for disposal.[1]

In this year the major decision was taken to leave Newcastle and the parent business and to establish the antiquarian branch of the firm in London. By June 1930, in the middle of a slump of unparalleled proportions, the brothers were established at 16 Pall Mall. Under such circumstances the move to the metropolis and the lavish fitting-out of premises in one of its most exclusive thoroughfares represented a considerable act of faith. The location was chosen in defiance of a good deal of well-meant advice; for, although Pall Mall had boasted several of the greatest bookselling houses a century earlier, by 1930 these had migrated further north to the area around Bond Street. Nevertheless the Robinsons persisted, because they had already discovered that from the point of view of *selling* books the venue was unimportant: whereas they rightly assessed Pall Mall as an excellent place for the *buying* of books.

For between the wars the pace at which ancient family libraries came on to the market perceptibly quickened, and it needed no clairvoyant to prophesy that supplies of rare books from such sources were not inexhaustible. But Messrs Robinson alone recast their business into a framework specially designed to attract dealings with the country gentleman; and the brothers soon realized that as a booksellers' work of reference Debrett was a formidable rival in usefulness to *Book-Auction Records*. Owners of great houses, they rightly argued, had London clubs and would value the accessibility of their Pall Mall address: and because no backwoodsman peer is wholly at his ease when he adopts the unfamiliar role of book seller they sought to minimize his embarrassment by providing discreet and familiar surroundings of sober mahogany and polished calf. The bound 'furnishing' sets which lined the shop at 16 Pall Mall, and which the casual visitor of

[1] Catalogues 18 (Early English Literature) and 19 (*Americana*).

modest means found so daunting, were in fact part of an elaborate and deliberately constructed setting. No such setting, however, would have availed had not the firm become widely recognized as one which paid fair prices for fine books. The extraordinary success of these methods cannot be better demonstrated than by the statement that in twenty-five years of trading the brothers succeeded in making private purchases from almost eighty members of the British peerage.

Nevertheless the early period in London was a lean one because of the depression, and the successful launching of the London business owed a good deal to the confidence and custom which it received in the first few years from two very well-known book collectors, Lord Rothschild and the late Sir Louis Sterling. The former visited 16 Pall Mall first as an undergraduate, and made an appropriate early purchase of a first issue of *Gulliver's Travels.* The house of Robinson bought largely for him in the auction-room and acted on his behalf in several important private transactions, such as the purchase of the Marquess of Headfort's copy of the Bristol *Lyrical Ballads.*[1] Sir Louis Sterling, whose collection[2] was given to the University of London in 1953, bought most of his finest books through the Robinsons' agency; and his constant friendship and wise counsel on financial affairs was of special value to the business. The year 1931 saw the first of a series of annual visits to the United States and the beginning of many personal relationships with great American collectors and librarians; in the same year Lionel visited Leningrad and succeeded in buying a number of fine books from the Soviet Government.[3] A considerable coup in the auction-room was achieved at the Peckover sale in July 1932, when two Syriac Biblical manuscripts of the fifth and sixth centuries were knocked down for under £200 to an astonished member of the firm who had come prepared to bid twenty times that figure for them.[4]

[1] *The Rothschild Library: a Catalogue,* II (1954), no. 2602.
[2] *The Sterling Library: a Catalogue* (1954).   [3] Described in Catalogue 39.
[4] Described in Catalogue 50 and purchased by the Pierpont Morgan Library at £3500.

A handful of examples must serve to chart the progress of the firm in the years preceding the Second World War. In March 1935 the brothers bought on Sir Louis Sterling's behalf the set of the four Shakespeare Folios consigned to Sotheby's by a Massachusetts institution; three years later they made important purchases from the muniment room of Loseley House, Surrey, among them dramatic documents of the time of Shakespeare, which passed into the Folger Shakespeare Library, an institution which also acquired from the same firm John Donne's original love-letters, after a fruitless attempt had been made by the Friends of the National Libraries to raise the sum of £2500 to retain them in this country. In 1939 they bought privately the very interesting library formed by George Grenville, the promoter of the Stamp Act of 1765, of which they issued a catalogue in 1940. Two books exercised a particular attraction over the brothers, Audubon's *Birds of America* and the first edition of King James's *Bible*, 1611, and in a quarter of a century a very high proportion of the copies which came on to the market passed through their hands.[1]

The qualities which the two brothers brought to the business made for a partnership of unusual harmony, for they were in large measure complementary, Lionel's more forceful personality and financial flair being nicely balanced by Philip's quieter and more academic demeanour. In the latter's responsibility for the firm's catalogues he was powerfully aided by the scholarship of Ralph Lewis, who for twenty-five years filled the role of manuscript expert to the business. Lewis was a bachelor, a self-taught and dedicated scholar, mordantly cynical at times of the commercial qualities of the treasures which he was cataloguing, a well-trusted member of the staff, privileged in the delivery of outspoken and uncompromising judgements; his share in the firm's success should not be underrated. The year 1939 saw the house of Robinson a highly personal and specialized business, well-known

[1] Prices paid for Audubon ranged from £500 in 1930 to £12,000 twenty-six years later: of the 1611 *Bible* the firm handled King James's own copy, as well as Prince Henry's and the copy from the Garter Chapel.

to all influential figures in the book-world, run on lines which diverged sharply from those of most antiquarian booksellers of similar status, though the brothers played their full share in the growth of the Antiquarian Booksellers' Association, of which Lionel was president in the difficult years 1938 to 1942.

The Second World War caused an almost complete cessation of business, but 16 Pall Mall did not close its doors, though some surrounding buildings were destroyed by bombs and the shop windows were twice blown in by blast. With the aid of Sir Basil Blackwell a house was found at Oxford in which Lewis and the best books were installed, and in 1945 the firm with its stock, staff and premises intact was in a sound position to take rapid advantage of the favourable trading conditions of the immediate post-war years. Henceforward the dominant key-note of the firm's business was quality, both in respect of the stock and the customers: and there was a grain of truth in the rumour circulated by rueful rivals that the Robinsons' clientele was becoming more and more confined to dukes and millionaires. The legend was to some degree fostered by the Lucullan entertainment which the brothers offered from time to time to groups of book-collectors, the most sumptuous of which occurred on 16 March 1949, when, at a dinner in honour of Mr Arthur Houghton and Mr Donald Hyde, the Duke of Gloucester and other notabilities were their guests at the Ritz.[1] It will thus be readily understood that temperamentally, if not financially, the firm was well equipped to pursue a project beyond the emulation of far larger and older-established houses, the purchase of the vast residue of Bibliotheca Phillippica.

The long-standing identification of the house of Sotheby with sales from the Phillipps Collection suggested first an approach to the Trustees through this channel, and after discussions with the late Major Felix Warre and G. D. Hobson the Robinson brothers in December 1944 offered the sum of £100,000 for the residue of the library and the Old Master drawings. Undeterred by the

[1] See Viscount Mersey's *Journal and Memories* (1952), p. 94.

refusal of this offer the brothers in the following month arranged a meeting with the life-tenant, Mr Alan Fenwick, and on 19 February 1945 they renewed their bid of £100,000 for the library alone, excluding the drawings.[1] Since they had the life-tenant's assurance that this figure would be the subject of the Trustees' serious consideration they began to explore at this stage methods of raising such a considerable sum. Their first thought was to contract to sell the entire manuscript collection at a modest advance, prior to purchase, retaining as their main source of profit the printed books, and on 8 March they announced by cable to Professor William A. Jackson of Harvard that they might be in a position to offer him the whole residue of the Phillipps manuscripts, about 12,000 in number, for £110,000. Jackson in his reply suggested that Harvard might provide a half-share of the purchase price and asked for more precise information on the number and nature of the manuscripts.

This information however was not available—even to the prospective purchasers. The whole library lay in crates in the cellars of Thirlestaine House and the only guide was a list of about five hundred and thirty of the best manuscripts compiled by Mr L. M. Irby, a member of Messrs Sotheby's staff, who made a probate valuation of the collection on FitzRoy Fenwick's death in 1938. On 4 April the brothers, accompanied by Mr Irby, visited the cellars and opened at random a cross-section of the boxes. They could see comparatively little, but sufficient to harden their resolution to bring the negotiation to a successful outcome. In a cable of 6 April and in a long letter of the same date they urged with all the earnestness they could command that Harvard should seize this unique opportunity, and they staked their professional reputation on the correctness of their estimate of the collection's value. Unhappily for Harvard, at this point Professor Jackson set off on a U.S. Government mission to South America

---

[1] This figure—after making an adjustment for the value of the drawings and deducting Messrs Sotheby's commission payable on the original offer—represented an advance of £23,000.

and was largely *incommunicado* for three months. Robbed of the advice of the man who could best appreciate the exceptional nature of the circumstances the University Librarian, Dr Keyes Metcalf, felt obliged to ask the Robinsons once again for more detailed information: and one can well appreciate that approach to a potential benefactor was fraught with great difficulty in default of any precise description of what Harvard was to expect for its £110,000. But, as the Robinsons replied on 11 April, it was literally impossible to add anything to their former communications, and on 14 April Metcalf cabled his regretful inability to accept. On 20 April the brothers made a similar approach to the British Museum, but there too the proposal was declined, though not for any lack of enthusiastic support from the Keeper of the Department of Manuscripts, who well recognized the unrivalled opportunity to enrich the national collection.

A lull of nearly six months followed during which the Fenwick Trustees made overtures to at least one other bookselling house, only to find that even the firm of Quaritch, doyen of the trade, was not disposed to contemplate a purchase of manuscripts on this scale; nor did the life-tenant's negotiations with the late Charles Stonehill come to fruition; and it should not fail to be recorded that the veteran collector, Sir Chester Beatty, made a brave but unsuccessful bid of £90,000 for the whole library. In the meantime the Robinsons were making strenuous efforts to raise the purchase price, and were brought face to face with one of the curiosities of banking, that whereas overdrafts can (or could then) be secured on diamonds, Gainsboroughs or combine harvesters, the great banking houses have little faith in books as security. Through the good offices of Sir Louis Sterling however the brothers were introduced to a merchant banking house prepared to take a less jaundiced view of the commercial potentialities of literature, and on 7 September 1945 they signed an agreement for an advance of £80,000. To the financiers the risk seemed substantial and this was properly reflected in their terms. To secure the loan the brothers had to produce £20,000 and in effect mortgage their business, stock and personal assets; they undertook moreover that any profits which accrued from marketing the Phillipps Collection should be shared equally with the bankers. When one recalls that ninety per cent of the library was unlisted and un-examined the boldness of the Robinsons' gamble becomes apparent. The conditional contract for its purchase at £100,000 was signed on 3 September 1945.

More than five anxious months however were still to elapse before the Court of Chancery set its *imprimatur* on the transaction. At a Court hearing on 13 December 1945 the sale of the Old Master Drawings to the British Museum was approved, but the Trustees' solicitors, Walker, Martineau and Co., requested further time to investigate the adequacy of the price of the library. Messrs Robinson were offered, and declined, an opportunity to sell the manuscripts on commission as the Trustees' agents, and the question of reserving some part of the collection from the sale[1] provided a further ground for debate and delay. It was not until 19 February 1946 that Mr Justice Wynn Parry finally gave the Court's consent to the sale.

Accommodation was at a premium in post-war London, and the housing of such a vast library in conditions where it could be examined was no easy problem. By good fortune it was possible to rent No. 1 Gordon Square from the University of London to contain the manuscripts; and the crypt of the neighbouring Catholic Apostolic Church was secured as a warehouse for the printed books. A substantial Victorian house at Barnet was also converted into book-stacks at a later date. On 27 March 1946 the first consignment of the best manuscripts reached London; on two days at the end of April further blocks of material were moved and the final conveyance of the great bulk of the collection began on 27 May when convoys of lorries, including six-wheelers with trailers, plied between Cheltenham and London for five days and nights.

[1] Twenty-nine manuscripts were in the event retained by the Trustees as a token of the collection and have been placed on deposit at the British Museum.

In the meantime negotiations with Harvard entered a second phase. Professor Jackson, released from Government service, had been making strenuous efforts to secure benefactions, and in March 1946 he renewed by cable the original proposition that Harvard should buy the entire collection. Circumstances however were now less favourable. The purchase price had, at some sacrifice, been raised elsewhere and the Robinsons were no longer the only parties interested in the disposal of the collection. A group of the most valuable manuscripts had already been earmarked for consignment to Messrs Sotheby, and it was therefore impossible to make any promise of selling the collection intact. After a brisk interchange of cables and letters Professor Jackson reached London on June 17, was given the key of No. 1 Gordon Square and spent a week going through the manuscripts. He has been kind enough to set down for me his recollections refreshed by reference to notes made at the time.

I was staggered by the amount of material there [he wrote on 18 September 1956], but I was also very much impressed by the fact that item after item was already published. For during the 19th century Phillipps and Fenwick had permitted scholars from Europe to come over and transcribe the manuscripts. That is particularly true of the French romances, and many of the classical texts, though there were, of course, important exceptions. It was apparent also that a number of very fine things had gone, including the ones in the Sotheby sale, among them a number of the items which Philip Hofer and I had seen in 1938 and had realized were the gems that Fenwick was then showing us. As a result of that visit I said we would not take the collection as a whole, for I had instructions from Harvard that I was to be able to say that this was of great scholarly import and not that they were beautiful manuscripts; i.e. that a large part of the collection were to be items that could be published by Harvard scholars or other scholars working here. On that basis I had to say no.

If Professor Jackson felt that, all things considered, the purchase was not one which he could urge upon his governing body he had no such doubts about the ultimate break-up value of the residue, and he has recalled how he told the brothers that they would in the not distant future bless the day on which he had declined to remove *en bloc* their hard-won treasure. And so in fact it turned out. The sale at Sotheby's on 1 July 1946, in which thirty-four of the finest manuscripts were offered, attracted energetic bidding from institutions and collectors starved during the war years of the opportunity to acquire items of the highest calibre: and the total realized, £55,190, represented a comfortable fraction of the purchase price of the whole collection. Three outstanding lots call for special mention; 13, a celebrated fourteenth-century volume of Provençal songs, decorated with miniature portraits of the troubadours (8335) was bought by Dr Rosenbach for £7500; Messrs Maggs paid £4800 on behalf of Dr Martin Bodmer for lot 22, a Renaissance manuscript of Vergil with twelve superb half-page miniatures (3506), and the same firm bought for £6200 lot 26A, an Aesop's *Fables* written in Italy about 1480 and illustrated with one hundred and thirty-five miniatures of great beauty and delicacy (23609: New York Public Library).

On 11 November 1946 one hundred and sixty-five lots of autograph letters and historical papers were auctioned at Sotheby's for a total of £19,740. Most important of these were lots 5–8, a large collection of official papers relating to the Colony of Georgia (14200–14220) which the State of Georgia secured for £4000. Sir Louis Sterling paid £1910 for lots 59 and 64, Marlborough's correspondence as commander-in-chief, together with a related series of battle plans, and handsomely presented the collection to the Duke's illustrious descendant, Sir Winston Churchill; and King Farouk bought for £2200 lot 68, eight folio volumes of Napoleonic documents and papers, many of them relating to Egypt. In a two-day sale beginning on 25 November three hundred and sixty-three lots of printed books from the Phillipps Collection were sold for £17,024, a considerable share of this total being contributed by the excellent prices realized by a large group of one of Phillipps's favourite lines of collecting, his Spanish and Portuguese romances.

Simultaneously with these three dispersals at Sotheby's some substantial sales were made privately. In the last three months of 1946 the National Maritime Museum, Greenwich, through the generosity of Sir James Caird, made four large purchases of naval papers for a total of £22,000. The late D. M. Colman of Hove paid £15,875 for nineteen manuscripts,[1] most of which were subsequently resold to Yale University Library. A few institutions[2] and private collectors[3] at this stage were concerned in transactions of a scale which was smaller than the foregoing but large by ordinary book-selling standards, and within a year of the original purchase the cost of the whole had been recovered by the sale of some of the most valuable items, while the vast bulk of the collection still remained largely unsorted and unexamined. At this point the Robinson brothers made the wise but expensive decision to recover their sole ownership and control of the library: and in June 1947 they repurchased the bankers' share of interest in the remainder.

Henceforth auction-sales played with one exception a decidedly minor role in the disposal of Phillipps material.[4] The exception was a pamphlet of extreme rarity which came to light among the vast masses of printed material, *The Journal of Major George Washington*, Williamsburg, 1754. No copy had appeared in the auction-room since 1880; hence the current market value of this pamphlet, of which only seven other surviving examples were known, was exceptionally difficult to assess. Sold by auction at the Parke-Bernet Galleries, New York, on 10 May 1955 it brought $25,000.

[1] Among them 3669 Boccaccio, and 13332 Livy.
[2] E.g. Victoria Public Library, Bibliothèque Royale, Brussels, Harvard University Library (2164 Vergil) and the Pierpont Morgan Library (3641 *Roy Modus*).
[3] E.g. Sir David Eccles, Mr Philip Hofer and the late J. W. Hely-Hutchinson.
[4] The following were the principal auctions at which Phillipps material was offered: Sotheby 19 Feb. 1947, lots 500–586, MSS. unsold at sales held before 1939; Hodgson 28 Nov. 1947; Sotheby 1 Dec. 1947, 131 lots, MSS.; Sotheby 21 March 1949, 283 lots, bibliography; Sotheby 28 Nov. 1949, lot 126, Moghul miniatures; Sotheby 13 Feb. 1950, 287 lots, printed books; Sotheby 12 June 1950; Hodgson 24 Jan. 1957, 591 lots, *Americana*; Hodgson 23 Jan. 1958, lots 419–486, bibliography.

Between 1948 and 1954 Messrs Robinson included a large number of greater and lesser items from the Phillipps Collection in their catalogues 77–84. Four of these catalogues call for particular mention. One of them[1] was devoted to the description of a single manuscript (No. 8336), the famous fourteenth-century volume containing eighty separate texts, over half of them unique, and almost the sole source of our knowledge of the work of the Anglo-Norman poet Nicholas Bozon.[2] This catalogue and two others (81 and 83), produced under the typographical supervision of Mr John Dreyfus of the Cambridge University Press, must rank for splendour of their contents, lavishness of illustration and opulence of production among the most costly and sumptuous catalogues ever issued by a bookseller. Pending the publication of the finding-list of Phillipps manuscripts it must suffice for the present to note a handful of the most valuable items which changed hands during this final phase, and the following incomplete list of four- and five-figure transactions will give some indication of the scale of the most recent operations.

Sir Chester Beatty acquired the splendid Armenian Gospels (15364) with which Phillipps had proudly been photographed in 1860. The late J. W. Hely-Hutchinson bought about a dozen manuscripts, including 16395, an early tenth-century text of Juvenal, 852, a copy of Lucian formerly owned by Grolier, and 6650, a beautiful Greek humanistic manuscript of the *Odyssey*. From Catalogue No. 77 the British Museum bought the twelfth-century Cartulary of Sherborne Abbey (3626). From the same catalogue Dr Martin Bodmer bought among other things the fine copy of the Gospels in Greek, written about A.D. 1000 (13975), the only known manuscript of the Anglo-Norman romance of *Waldef* (8345), and also (through Mr Heinrich Eisemann) the famous Babylonian clay cylinder of Nebuchadnezzar recording about 595 B.C. the rebuilding of Babylon. Dr Bodmer's further purchases were of great value and importance, including 17849,

---

[1] No. 79 in the series.
[2] Now BM. Add. MS. 46919.

a collection of canons and decretals written in a variety of eighth-century North Italian hands, 6547–8, a two-volume manuscript, the earliest known, of a large portion of the Latin version of Josephus, written in the second half of the eighth century,[1] 16069, the Gradual of the monastery of Saint Cecilia at Rome, signed and dated 1071 and containing the earliest known example of pre-Gregorian chant,[2] and 3111, a splendidly illuminated copy of Boccaccio's *Des Cas de Nobles Hommes et Femmes*, written at Tours about 1475.[3]

Mr Arthur Houghton bought 3715, the twelfth-century *Mappae Clavicula*, for the Corning Museum of Glass, the Pierpont Morgan Library 8297, a noble text of Pliny's *Natural History* written about 830 at the monastery of St Nazarius at Lorsch, near Worms, Harvard University a tenth-century Horace (15363), the University of Oregon 26092, *Geste de Montglane*, and the Thomas Gilcrease Foundation at Tulsa, Oklahoma, 20994, the autograph journal of Luke Foxe during his voyage in search of a North-West Passage in 1631.[4] Another naval manuscript of even greater romantic interest was 25342, a group of papers relating to the Spanish Armada, including Philip of Spain's autograph instructions to the Duke of Medina Sidonia, which appropriately passed to the National Maritime Museum. Sir David Eccles bought the papers of Sir Robert Ker Porter, rich in South American interest,[5] the Caird Trustees 6448, the Armagnac manuscript of the trials of Joan of Arc,[6] and the Public Record Office 4099, a volume of accounts relating to the fabric of the Palace of Westminster 1307–11. Among outstanding printed books from the Phillipps Collection the sale to the Duke of Northumberland of Caxton's first publication, the *Recuyell of the Historyes of Troy*, Bruges, 1475, must be recorded.

These substantial sales of Phillipps material, matched by several

[1] Catalogue 83, pp. 76–8. [2] Catalogue 83, pp. 58–62.
[3] Catalogue 81, item 17. [4] Catalogue 77, item 84.
[5] Resold at Sotheby's 4 Nov. 1957, lots 168–184.
[6] Catalogue 83, pp. 71–5.

transactions on a similar scale involving books from other sources, brought a high degree of prosperity to the firm. Two pieces of good fortune had contributed to this end. The brothers had outbid all rivals for the Phillipps Collection just before the post-war inflationary trend had fully revealed itself, and they were therefore in the happy position of meeting a world of sharply rising prices with a stock of unexampled extent and richness. Moreover devaluation of the pound sterling resulted, designedly, in increased American buying of British goods of all kinds, and added a stimulus to the operations of those collectors and libraries across the Atlantic which formed a major fraction of the Robinsons' clientele.

This great expansion however laid a heavy burden on the two partners, a burden increased by the sudden death of Ralph Lewis in June 1956. Neither of the brothers had a male heir and there was therefore no good family reason to maintain the business at a tempo which was becoming increasingly onerous. The stock and goodwill were of great value but the highly personal nature of the business made its sale fraught with particular difficulty. Potential purchasers stipulated the continued activity of the brothers in fostering the relationships with sellers and buyers of books which had brought such success to the firm, and having set their hearts upon retirement this was a stipulation to which the Robinsons could not agree: and so it came about in December 1956 that the house of William H. Robinson Ltd. closed its doors.

On their retirement the brothers retained, in their new capacity of private owners, the residue of the Phillipps Collection, still extensive and of infinite variety. The routine commitments of commerce had allowed all too little time for the patient examination of many thousands of manuscripts and documents, which at a cursory view had seemed to be of secondary importance, and a good deal of the brothers' newly found leisure has been devoted to winnowing the wheat from the chaff. The orderly segregation of what is valuable and the jettisoning of the worthless will occupy

PHILIP AND LIONEL ROBINSON

a good many years yet, but one of the first-fruits of the brothers' new activity has been seen in their generous presentation to the Bodleian Library of the whole of Sir Thomas's personal papers, on which these *Phillipps Studies* have been based. Placed alongside Madden's journals, to which they are complementary, they will provide a rich mine of information on bookselling, book-collecting and scholarship in the nineteenth century.

It would be premature at this stage to trace the history of the Phillipps Library any further. The formation and dispersal of the collection has so far covered nearly a century and a half, over a third of the period during which private libraries have been formed in England. Phillipps was twenty at the time of the Roxburghe sale, and the narrative spans book-collecting from Heber to Harmsworth and beyond, and bookselling from Payne and Foss, who had their roots in the eighteenth century, to that other establishment in Pall Mall with which the story ends. At the outset of our chronicle five pounds bought a manuscript worth as many hundreds today, although conversely certain classes of topographical material would command prices now which compare unfavourably with their value a century ago. In our period we have seen the Public Records, for which Phillipps cared so passionately, reduced to comparative order from the formless and neglected jumble in which he found them in his youth. The history of scholarship from Sir Richard Colt Hoare onwards has been a central part of our theme and many of its greatest names have appeared in our pages, not to mention a number of those picturesque figures of the scholarly *demi-monde*— Halliwell with his tarnished reputation and downright rogues and charlatans such as Libri and Simonides. We have touched upon the bitter sectarian quarrels which divided England in the nineteenth century and the appearances in our narrative of Catlin and Fox Talbot have impinged upon the history of subjects as diverse as ethnology and photography. The personal affairs of Sir Thomas himself and of Sir Frederic Madden have furnished episodes of poignant human interest, a relief to the writer and, one hopes, to the reader among the overlong chronicle of acquisition and dispersal.

The dispersal is now world-wide. In private collections, libraries, record offices and bookshops in most countries of the Western world are to be found fragments of the vast library which Phillipps amassed with such dedicated zeal: and if, as a result of these *Phillipps Studies*, collectors, booksellers, librarians and scholars, when confronted with one of Sir Thomas's accession-numbers on a fly-leaf, think with heightened interest and understanding of the extraordinary architect of Bibliotheca Phillippica, I shall feel rewarded for labours which have occupied my leisure for more than a dozen years.

ADDITIONS AND CORRECTIONS
TO PHILLIPPS STUDIES NOS. I–4

p. 1, n. 1. Students of the Middle Hill Press will also need to consult Mr Harrison D. Horblit, 79 Madison Avenue, New York, who has assembled, with the aid of the Robinson brothers, a very extensive collection of works from the Press, especially rich in proof-sheets.

p. 2, n. 4. Messrs Robinson's copy of the 1819 catalogue is now in the possession of Major J. R. Abbey.

p. 9, l. 25. *For* p. 187 *read* p. 187* [note in Madden's copy of *Catalogus Librorum Manuscriptorum*].

p. 13. *After para.* 2 *insert*: A considerably expanded edition of the catalogue was planned and one sheet of it was printed in 1842. It is headed CATALOGUS / LIBRORUM MANUSCRIPTORUM / in BIBLIOTHECA MEDIOMONTANA / D. THOMAE PHILDIPPS [*sic*], Bart. / 1842. Folio, 4 pp. Fourteen manuscripts are described, each with a substantial number of sub-headings. The only copy I have seen is a proof, much corrected in Phillipps's hand, which belonged to the Earl of Ashburnham. I bought it from Mr H. W. Pratley of Tunbridge Wells in 1953, soon after he had purchased the residue of the Ashburnham Library.

p. 17, l. 22. *For* six *read* seven [photostats of *Catalogus Librorum Manuscriptorum*].
   l. 25. *After* Grolier Club *add* and the Henry E. Huntington Library.

p. 19, n. 4. Dr Bernhard Bischoff has pointed out that Phillipps was not in error. The fifth-century Pauline Epistles once at Clermont (now Bibliothèque Nationale Grec. 107) contained two palimpsest leaves of the *Phaethon* of Euripides in fourth-century uncials. It passed however from Clermont long before Meerman's time, having been bought by Louis XIV for the Royal Library before 1656. See *C.L.A.* Part V, No. 521.

p. 24, Census No. 10. *For* Indexes lacking *read* Indexes now complete.
Add 10 A. CHICAGO, Newberry Library.
Complete

p. 25. *Add* 12 A. DURHAM, University Library.
Index to Part 1; Dr Martin Routh's copy (No. 66).
Add 14 A. THE HAGUE, Royal Library.
Almost complete; Viscount Strangford's copy (No. 70).
No. 17. *For* no indexes *read* index to Part 1 only.

p. 27, No. 28. This copy is now owned by the late Mr Goodhart's
daughter, Mrs John D. Gordan, 113 East 78th St., New York. It
lacks thirty-four leaves from the body of the catalogue and nine
from the indexes.

p. 32. *Add* 59 A. EARL OF MUNSTER.
According to a note in Henrietta Phillipps's diary in the
possession of Mr E. Walcot Bather the Earl of Munster was
sent pp. 13–40, 45–6 and 49–96*.
No. 63. *For* 3 May 1863 *read* 3 May 1862.
No. 65. This copy was in lot 135 E at the Hengrave Hall sale on
15 September 1952 and was acquired by Messrs Robinson.

p. 33, No. 66. Delete entry (now 12 A).
No. 67. *For* N. Piers *read* H. Piers.
No. 70. Delete entry (now 14 A).
No. 71. *For* W. C. Pettigrew *read* T. J. Pettigrew.
The Sussex copy was lot 2412 in the sale of the first part of the
library of L. L. Hartley at Puttick's on 1 June 1885. Hartley also
owned Viscount Strangford's copy (P. 1 June 1885, lot 2411) and
Madden's copy (P. 3 May 1886, lot 563 (179) and 18 April 1887,
lot 436). I am much obliged to Mr D. D. Evans for drawing my
attention to this catalogue. The annotated entries of Hartley's
extensive collection of Middle Hill Press books are a useful source
of bibliographical information.

p. 35. To the census of copies of the catalogue of MSS. add the
following fragmentary copies, more or less heavily perfected with
photostats, which have been supplied to the undermentioned
libraries by Messrs Robinson since 1951.
CHICAGO, Newberry Library.
DUBLIN, National Library of Ireland.
NEW YORK, Pierpont Morgan Library.

PENNSYLVANIA, University Library.
PHILADELPHIA, Free Library.
PRINCETON, University Library.
CHARLOTTESVILLE, VIRGINIA, Alderman Library.
YALE, University Library.

p. 39. Copies 3 and 4 in the census of the catalogue of printed books have passed into the possession of the Newberry Library, Chicago, and of Mr D. P. Wheatland, Cambridge, Mass.

p. 40. To the census of copies of the *Catalogue of Printed Books* add:
9 CAMBRIDGE, MASS., Philip Hofer.
Complete, bought from E. P. Goldschmidt and Co., 1954.

. Mr Philip Robinson has brought to light an octavo issue of Supplements 2–4. It bears a drop-title: CATALOGUE OF BOOKS AT MIDDLEHILL. 2nd Supplement. 3rd Supplement, 1841. 4th Supplement, 1841. Printed on 48 pages it contains printed books Nos. 4575 to 5557. He has also found a single copy of a folio title-page for a projected catalogue of incunabula: CATALOGUS / INCUNABULORUM / IN / BIBLIOTHECA / MEDIO-MONTANA. / [rule] / TYPIS / MEDIOMONTANIS.

NO. 2

p. 1, l. 15. *After* his only son was born *add* at 32 Cannon St., Manchester.

p. 2, l. 5. *For* Phillips *read* Phillipps.

p. 28, l. 9. *For* Phillipp *read* Phillipps. Mr P. Glazebrook has pointed out that this was Robert Biddulph Phillipps of Longworth, Barrister of the Middle Temple, book-collector and antiquary, who having been converted to Roman Catholicism left his library to Belmont Priory (now Abbey) on his death in 1864. The choicest items from this library were sold at Sotheby's in July 1954.

p. 29, l. 2 and n. 1. *For* Sir William Gore Ouseley *read* Sir Gore Ouseley.

p. 34. Mr Irvine E. Gray, Records Officer to the Gloucestershire County Council, has drawn my attention to the Apperley Court Records which contain correspondence between Phillipps and members of the Strickland family relating to a match between Hugh Strickland and Henrietta Phillipps. Mr Gray writes: 'It appears that between Nov. 1839 and June 1840 Hugh Strickland, the naturalist, son of Henry Eustachius Strickland of Apperley, wished to pay his addresses to Sir Thomas Phillipps's elder daughter Henrietta, but never actually got as far as this, becauses Sir Thomas' financial requirements (before he would allow any approach to his daughter) were so drastic. Actually the Stricklands were prepared to fall in with his demands to the extent of giving a bond for £40,000 to pay all Sir Thomas's debts in the event of his not having an heir (he says he intends to remarry) and of Henrietta's succeeding in consequence to the entailed estates.

'There are in all 25 letters and draft letters between the Stricklands father and son, and Sir Thomas, including nine from the latter. Sir Thomas suddenly breaks off negotiations without any proper explanation, leaving the Stricklands very puzzled and somewhat annoyed, not unnaturally....From your book it seems evident that Sir Thomas's motive in choking off the Stricklands was his wish to marry Henrietta to Sir Henry Dryden.'

p. 64, n. 1. My tentative identification of 'Mr Dighton' is almost certainly wrong. Phillipps was probably addressing the local artist of this name from whom he commissioned a drawing of Sir Frederic Madden.

p. 87, l. 14 and n. 2. *For* Sparkes *read* Sparks.

p. 97, l. 24. *For* Mr *read* My.

p. 101, l. 7. *For* John F. A. Fenwick *read* John E. A. Fenwick.
Last line. *For* bequest *read* devise.

NO. 3

p. 28, n. 1. On the Musschenbroek sale see *Folium*, III, 3/4 (1954), pp. 115–22.

p. 33, l. 9. *For* Giambista *read* Giambattista.

p. 46, n. 2. Messrs Harding, Triphook and Lepard issued a catalogue in 1824. Triphook subsequently joined the firm of Lackington, Harding and Co.

p. 59, n. 1. *For* 4 July 1830 *read* 6 July 1830.

p. 61, n. 9. Mr Neil Ker assures me that the group of MSS. from English monasteries at Trinity College, Oxford, is a notable one.

p. 68, last line. *For* 1827 *read* 1826 [date of Phillipps's parliamentary candidature].

p. 72, l. 24. For *Catalogus Manuscriptorum* read *Catalogus Librorum Manuscriptorum.*

p. 74, l. 6. By 'Donan' Phillipps means Pierre Charles François Daunou.

p. 75, n. 1. Mr Arthur Cole has pointed out that the sentence 'Dibdin was an executor, but subsequently resigned the office' is legally unacceptable. *Read* 'Dibdin was appointed an executor but subsequently renounced the office'.

p. 88, l. 11. *For* Burleigh *read* Burghley.

p. 95, n. 1. *For* William Coombe *read* William Combes of Henley.

p. 96, l. 5. *For* sixteen *read* twenty-six. I am indebted for this correction to Dr B. Lawn of Barnes, who owns a very extensive collection of Thorpe's catalogues.

p. 121, l. 11. *For* Bridges *read* Brydges.

p. 127, l. 9. Phillipps also sent Curzon a copy of Le Gallois's *Traitté des plus belles bibliothèques de l'Europe*, 1685. The original copy with Curzon's note of the presentation was given to me in 1954 by Major J. R. Abbey.

p. 154, l. 4. Thomas Barrett of Lee Priory is another possible identification of this provenance.

p. 157, l. 27. Professor W. A. Jackson has pointed out that *ex Bibl. Petri Thomson, Equitis* refers to the friend of Ames, Sir Peter Thompson, whose books and manuscripts appeared in five sales between 1815 and 1852.

p. 158, last entry. Professor W. A. Jackson writes: 'The Rev. Henry White's books were privately offered for sale in 1824 in the second part of Harding, Triphook and Lepard's catalogue. The preface of this, which tells of the Rev. Mr White, is dated July 6th 1824 and contains numbers 9804 to 15206. A copy of this catalogue is in my possession.'

p. 161, l. 2. *For* [? Petri] Prowse *read* W. Prouse. I owe this correction to Mr Godfrey Davis.

p. 169, l. 17. To my tentative identifications of 'Glynn' Mr D. D. Evans has added the more probable one of Richard Glynn, Bookseller, 36 Pall Mall.

NO. 4

p. xiii, l. 22. *For* Leeven *read* Leveen.

p. 4, l. 15. Lilly had started business on his own at least as early as February 1829 at 20 Henrietta Street, Covent Garden, moving to 3 Museum Street in the first half of 1830 (information kindly supplied by Mr D. D. Evans from Lilly's catalogues).

p. 15, l. 19. *For* 1773 *read* 1791 [Pettigrew's birth].

p. 19, l. 28. Mr John Warner, formerly Borough Librarian of Newport, Monmouthshire, tells me that the Newport Reference Library contains another substantial block of Sir Charles Hanbury Williams's papers.

p. 20, n. 1. Mr Warren R. Dawson points out that 'Mr Cureton' is wrongly identified. He was almost certainly Harry Osborne Cureton (1785–1858) who carried on a business as a dealer in manuscripts and antiquities at 81 Aldersgate.

p. 24. Here should be inserted a note of another great opportunity missed by Phillipps. On 9 June 1852 Messrs Hodges and Smith wrote from Dublin asking whether he was disposed to buy the famous 'Book of Armagh', the Gospels in Irish written in 807, now at Trinity College, Dublin. Phillipps replied on 11 June stating that 'the loss of £1,000 per annum through Free Trade puts me *hors de combat*'. Nevertheless he went on to inquire the price, but I have found no further correspondence on the subject.

p. 77, n. 2. *Add* See also Mr Doyle's 'Martin Joseph Routh and his books in Durham University Library', in *Durham University Journal*, June 1956, pp. 100–7.

p. 90, n. 1. *Add* My identification of Phillipps's unwelcome guest with James Wallis Pycroft is confirmed. His genealogical notes, made at Middle Hill and elsewhere, were lot 1523 in the third part of the L. L. Hartley sale at Puttick's on 18 April 1887.

pp. 95–6. Mr Anthony Hobson has identified the 'folio missal, executed for the Cardinal Julius de Medicis'. It was lot 443 in the

Hamilton Palace sale of 1882 and is now in Berlin, Kupferstich-Kabinett 78 D 17. See Paul Wescher, *Beschreibendes Verzeichnis der Miniaturen-Handschriften u. Einzelblätter des Kupferstich-Kabinetts* (Berlin, 1931), p. 104. The manuscript is in the hand of Arrighi.

p. 130, n. 3. 'Prince' Demetrius Rhodocanakis was a well-known impostor and forger. See Otto Kurz, *Fakes* (1948), pp. 71–2.
n. 4. *For* Ritsch *read* Ritschl.

p. 135, penultimate line. *For* forty-five *read* fifty-six.

p. 156, l. 25. *For* August *read* Augustus.

p. 159, l. 24. *For* Radcliffe Infirmary *read* Radcliffe Library.

p. 161, l. 19. I have followed Phillipps's error in ascribing the provenance of the five Lombardic books to Nuova Fossa: they came in fact from Nonantola.

p. 162, n. 10. *Add* Now B.M. Add. MS. 48984.

p. 211, ll. 26–8. *For* 23825 *read* 23835. *Add* or Ebenezer West, for whom see p. 139.

p. 215, n. 1. *For* William *read* Willard.

p. 221, n. 1. The Zuccaro drawings were bought by Dr A. S. W. Rosenbach and, together with the volume of ornaments by Giulio Romano referred to on p. 222, are now in the Rosenbach Foundation, Philadelphia.

pp. 226–7. The drawings listed as not found in 1946 have subsequently come to light among the residue of the Phillipps Collection and were presented to the British Museum by Lionel and Philip Robinson in 1957.

NUMERICAL INDEX
TO PHILLIPPS MANUSCRIPTS

5303	**5** 58	6845–6864	**3** 98, 162, 167, 168
6339	**5** 89n.	6865–6872	**3** 162
6358	**5** 63	6914	**3** 94, 137, 162
6448	**3** 56; **5** 109	6949	**3** 51, 153, 155
6453	**4** 206	7021	**3** 97
6460–6489	**3** 159	7022	**3** 97
6477	**4** 99n.	7023–7030	**3** 96, 162, 167
6490–6518	**3** 159	7031–7098	**3** 162
6519–6521	**3** 159	7099–7111	**3** 98, 162; **4** 191,
6522–6530	**3** 159		202
6531–6545	**3** 159, 169	7112–7403	**3** 162
6538	**4** 46	7294	**5** 57
6546–6549	**3** 94, 159	7404–7413	**3** 162
6546	**5** 73n.	7414–7441	**3** 162, 164
6547–8	**3** 94n.; **5** 109	7442–7446	**3** 162
6550–6569	**3** 94, 160, 166	7447	**3** 162
6570–6576	**3** 160	7448–7871	**3** 154, 159, 161, 162,
6577–6625	**3** 96, 160, 165		163, 166, 168; **4** 186,
6626	**3** 160		202, 206, 210
6627–6630	**3** 160	7872	**3** 163; **4** 188
6631	**3** 160	7873–7880	**3** 163
6632–6638	**3** 138, 160	7881–7890	**3** 163
6639–6655	**3** 160	7891–8069	**3** 163
6650	**5** 108	8025 [*bis*]	**5** 66, 69
6656–6667	**3** 160	8070–8497	**1** 1; **3** 78, 163
6668–6673	**3** 160	8074	**5** 62
6674–6690	**3** 85n., 160	8079	**5** 59
6691	**3** 160	8122	**5** 64
6692–6693	**3** 161	8135	**5** 63
6694–6733	**3** 92, 161	8214	**5** 85
6734–6737	**3** 154, 159, 161, 166,	8297	**3** 80 n.; **5** 109
	168; **4** 186, 202, 206,	8335	**5** 106
	210	8336	**2** 34; **3** 78n.; **4** 41;
6736	**3** 138		**5** 108
6738–6750	**3** 161	8345	**5** 198
6751–6755	**3** 161	8357	**5** 61
6756–6782	**3** 25, 144, 148, 150,	8397–8398	**3** 169
	161; **4** 175, 178, 189,	8400	**5** 73n.
	207, 208	8462	**5** 89
6783–6821	**3** 99, 161	8498–8511	**3** 164
6822–6828	**3** 161	8512–8515	**3** 164
6829–6832	**3** 161	8516	**3** 162, 164
6833–6835	**3** 33, 146, 157, 161	8517	**3** 164
6836	**3** 161	8518–8533	**3** 164
6837–6839	**3** 161	8534	**3** 164
6840	**3** 161	8535	**3** 164
6841–6843	**3** 161	8536	**3** 164
6844	**3** 161	8537–8538	**3** 164

10658	3 56, 159, 169	11622	4 174, 175, 183, 197, 203
10659–10705	3 165, 167, 169		
10706	3 169	11623–11631	4 175
10707	3 169	11632–11651	4 13, 175, 176, 177, 182, 184, 188, 189, 197, 198, 199
10708–10709	3 169		
10710	3 169		
10711–10817	3 156, 169	11652–11658	4 175
10818–10830	4 172	11659–11660	4 19, 173, 174, 175
10831–10842	4 19, 172, 185	11661	4 176, 190
10843–10844	4 172	11662–11669	4 176
10845–10854	4 172	11670–11684	4 176
10855–10860	4 172	11685–11687	4 15, 173, 174, 176, 196, 197, 199, 200, 206
10861–10873	4 173		
10874	4 173	11688	4 176
10875	4 173	11689	4 176
10876–10944	4 19, 173, 174, 175	11690	4 176
10945–11035	4 173	11691–11710	4 13, 175, 176, 177, 182, 184, 188, 189, 197, 198, 199
11036–11041	4 173		
11042–11082	4 173		
11083–11158	4 173	11711–11714	4 176
11122	4 162; 5 61	11715–11718	4 20, 174, 176, 211
11159–11256	4 15, 173, 174, 176, 196, 197, 199, 200, 206	11719–11726	4 176
		11727	4 176
		11728–11729	4 177
11257	4 173	11730	4 177
11258–11300	4 15, 173, 174, 176, 196, 197, 199, 200, 206	11731	4 177
		11732	4 177
11301	4 174	11733–11775	4 15, 175, 177, 180, 190, 205
11302–11305	4 174, 175, 183, 197, 203		
		11753	5 57
11306	4 174	11776–11780	4 177
11307–11328	4 20, 174, 176, 211	11781	4 177
11329–11373	4 174	11782	4 177
11374–11410	4 19, 173, 175	11783–11787	4 177, 205
11374–11399	4 174	11788–11794	4 18, 177, 186
11400–11410	4 174	11792	4 164; 5 61
11411–11412	4 15, 173, 174, 176	11793	4 18
11413	4 174	11795–11804	4 13, 175, 176, 177, 182, 184, 188, 189, 197, 198, 199
11414–11520	4 174		
11521–11581	4 174		
11582–11585	4 15, 175, 178, 179, 184, 189	11805–11807	4 177
		11808–11809	4 178
11586–11599	4 175	11810–11811	4 178
11600–11604	4 15, 175, 177, 180, 190, 205	11812–11814	4 15, 175, 178, 179, 184, 189, 207, 208
11605–11612	4 15, 175, 178, 179, 184, 189, 207, 208	11815–11819	4 178
		11820	4 178
11613–11621	4 175	11821–11826	4 178

13423–13424	**4** 183	13832–13833	**4** 82, 180, 186, 198, 203, 206, 211
13425–13427	**4** 183		
13428–13438	**4** 183	13834	**4** 186
13439–13446	**4** 17, 180, 183, 189	13835–13841	**4** 186
13447–13449	**4** 183	13842	**4** 186
13450–13452	**4** 183	13843	**4** 186; **5** 61
13453–13454	**4** 183	13844–13853	**4** 186
13455	**4** 183	13854	**4** 186, 202, 206, 210
13456–13495	**4** 19, 183, 184, 191	13855	**4** 186
13496	**4** 183	13856	**4** 186
13497	**4** 183	13857–13863	**4** 186
13498	**4** 183	13864–13885	**4** 127, 187
13499–13515	**4** 74n., 182, 183, 185	13877	**4** 127, 163
13516	**4** 174, 175, 183, 197, 203	13878	**4** 128
		13879	**4** 127
13517–13518	**4** 184	13880	**4** 127
13519–13525	**4** 19, 183, 184, 191	13881	**4** 127
13526	**4** 184	13886	**4** 187
13527–13528	**4** 184	13887–13889	**4** 187
13529–13530	**4** 184	13890	**4** 187, 192, 193, 201, 202
13531–13541	**4** 184		
13542–13593	**4** 184	13891–13892	**4** 187
13594–13624	**4** 184	13892	**4** 162
13625–13639	**4** 184	13893–13895	**4** 187
13640–13654	**4** 184	13896–13909	**4** 187
13655–13672	**4** 15, 175, 178, 179, 184, 189	13910–13927	**4** 136n., 187, 189, 205, 206
13673–13682	**4** 19, 183, 184, 191	13928–13929	**4** 187
13683–13694	**4** 13, 175, 176, 177, 182, 184, 188, 189, 197, 198, 199	13930	**4** 187
		13931	**4** 187
		13932	**4** 187
13695–13699	**4** 185	13933–13939	**4** 187
13700–13718	**4** 185, 191, 194	13940–13944	**4** 13, 175, 176, 182, 184, 188, 189, 197, 198
13719–13720	**4** 185		
13721–13745	**4** 19, 172, 185	13945–13949	**4** 188
13746–13751	**4** 185	13950	**4** 188
13752–13757	**4** 72, 181, 185, 193	13951	**4** 188
13758–13789	**4** 65, 180, 181, 185, 188, 208	13952–13953	**4** 188
		13954–13961	**4** 188
13790–13796	**4** 185	13962	**4** 188
13797–13804	**4** 74n., 182, 183, 185	13963–13964	**4** 65, 180, 181, 185, 188, 208
13805–13827	**4** 185	13965	**4** 188
13823	**4** 19; **5** 63	13966–13974	**4** 188
13828	**4** 185	13975–13976	**4** 188
13829	**4** 18n., 177, 186	13975	**4** 162; **5** 108
13830	**4** 186	13977–13979	**4** 188
13831	**4** 186	13980–13992	**4** 188

18576–18747	4 203
18748	4 203
18749–18795	4 203
18796–18797	4 82, 180, 186, 198, 203, 206, 211
18797	5 87
18798–19276	4 203
18833	4 161
18992	4 222
19277–19280	4 203
19281–19287	4 84, 204, 211
19288–19296	4 204
19297–19321	4 204
19322–19350	4 135, 204
19351–19365	4 204
19366–19379	4 204
19380–19586	4 204
19431–19478	4 135
19501–19586	4 135
19587–19591	4 204
19592–19642	4 204
19643–19695	4 135, 204
19696–19742	4 204
19743–19749	4 135, 204
19750–20000	4 204
20001–20167	4 204
20168–20182	4 135, 204
20183–20198	4 75, 189, 190, 193, 194, 198, 200, 204, 211
20199–20209	4 84, 192, 205
20210–20306	4 205
20307–20310	4 205
20311–20366	4 136, 205
20367–20417	4 205
20418–20420	4 205
20421–20536	4 135, 205
20537–20538	4 189, 191, 205
20539–20551	4 205
20552–20554	4 177, 205
20555–20581	4 205
20582–20586	4 205
20587–20604	4 136, 187, 189, 205, 206
20605–20641	4 205
20642–20643	4 73, 182, 190, 205
20644–20656	4 15, 175, 177, 180, 190, 205
20657–20682	4 135, 205

20677	4 222
20683–20684	4 205
20685–20694	4 82, 180, 186, 198, 203, 206, 211
20695–20762	4 206
20763–20788	4 15n., 173, 174, 196, 197, 199, 200, 206
20789	4 135, 206
20790–20809	4 136, 187, 189, 205, 206
20810–20962	4 206
20821	5 87
20963–20975	4 135, 206
20976–20989	4 206
20990–20992	4 206
20993–21043	4 206
20994	4 163; 5 109
21044–21070	4 135, 206
21070	4 209
21071–21151	4 186, 202, 206, 210
21152–21161	4 76, 193, 195, 196, 198, 200, 203, 206, 208, 210
21162–21183	4 206
21184–21189	4 206
21190–21230	4 206
21231–21357	4 138, 207, 210
21358–21397	4 207
21398–21427	4 207, 210
21428–21467	4 207
21468–21486	4 207
21487–21535	4 207
21536	4 175, 178, 189, 207, 208
21537–21606	4 207
21607–21615	4 207, 210
21616–21619	4 202, 203, 207
21620–21925	4 207
21708	5 63
21787	4 162; 5 72
21867	5 61
21926	4 207
21927–21941	4 75, 200, 201, 207, 208
21942–21968	4 207
21969–21972	4 207
21973–21974	4 175, 178, 189, 207, 208
21975–21988	4 208

GENERAL INDEX
TO THE WHOLE WORK

BIBLE (*cont.*)
New Testament
Latin
  eleventh century, with Bede's
    commentary, **5** 60
  unspecified MSS., **3** 173
English, Tyndale, **4** 97
Anglo-Saxon, **3** 128
Coptic, **4** 151
Welsh, 1567, **4** 97
Gospels
  Greek: ninth-century uncials, **4**
    100, 100n.; tenth century, **3** 61;
    4 162; eleventh century, **4** 162;
    5 108; Codex Leicesteriensis, **3**
    128; unspecified, **3** 170, 172,
    173, 174, 175, 176
  Latin: Ada MS. (eighth–ninth
    century), **3** 20, 20n.; Macdur-
    nan Gospels, **3** 128n.; ninth
    century, **3** 138; tenth century,
    4 95, 95n.; *c.* A.D. 1000 Stavelot
    Abbey, **5** 72; eleventh century,
    3 132
  Arabic, **3** 175
  Armenian, **4** ix, 163; **5** 108
  Bulgarian, **3** 132, 175
  Franco-Saxon, ninth century, **5** 72
  German, eleventh-century illumi-
    nated, **3** 138; **5** 70
  Irish, ninth-century *Book of
    Armagh*, **5** 118
  Italian, eleventh century, **5** 53
  Syriac, **5** 25
Acts and Epistles
  (with Apocalypse), **3** 173
  eleventh century, **3** 127
  unspecified, **3** 174
  Acts: Greek, **3** 172; Icelandic—
    Codex Scardensis, **4** 162
  Epistles: fifth century from Cler-
    mont, **5** 113; unspecified, **3** 175
Apocalypse
  Greek, twelfth or thirteenth cen-
    tury, **3** 128
  unspecified, **3** 171, 172
Biblical literature, **4** 15; **5** 42, 46, 47
Bibliographer's Manual, The, **1** 1

*Bibliographical Catalogue of Books
  Privately Printed*, **1** 1
Bibliographical Society of America,
  4 13n.
Bibliography, **1** 9; **4** 156; **5** 107n., 114
Biblioteca Real, **1** 31; **3** 149; **4** 100–1
Biblioteca Vittorio Emanuele, Rome,
  4 161n.
Bibliotheca Casanatense, Rome, **5** 31n.
Bibliotheca Lindesiana, **1** 35; **5** 66
Bibliotheca Phillippica
  accessions
    up to 1840, vol. **3** *passim*
    from 1841, to 1872 vol. **4** *passim*
  catalogues, vol. **1** *passim* (*catalogues
    are indexed under their various
    titles*)
    Preface to Catalogue of Manu-
      scripts (*c.* 1828), **1** 18–20
  descriptions of
    by F. W. Maitland to the Cam-
      bridge Senate, **5** 44
    by Rosenbach, **5** 77
    by Heinrich Schenkl, **5** 66n.
    by Gunnar Tilander, **5** 76
  disposal at Phillipps's death, **2** 101,
    106, 107, 108, 113–14
  under the Fenwicks
    abortive negotiations for the sale
      of MSS. to the British Museum,
      Oxford and Cambridge, **5** 42–50
    admission to the library, **5** 65–7,
      66n., 93
    affidavits on the library to the
      Court of Chancery, **5** 20–1
    exploratory moves for selling resi-
      due *en bloc*, **5** 95–6
    fees charged for consulting it, **5**
      16–19, 29, 44, 66
    Fenwick's valuation, **5** 16
    leave to sell the manuscripts
      granted, **5** 21
    letters of introduction to, **5** 17–18,
      66
    offers to the Trustees for the resi-
      due, **5** 101–3
    proposals for its support, **5** 15,
      16–17

145

British Museum (*cont.*)
Phillipps complains of lack of publication by, **3** 37
purchases
Bliss letters, **4** 80, 81
Samuel Butler's collection, **3** 109
R. W. Eyrton's MSS., **4** 203
letters of Sir John Fastolf, **5** 87n.
1603 *Hamlet*, **2** 116, 117
from Heber sale, **3** 77, 81
Mexican MSS., **4** 67
from Madden's collection (Egerton MS. 2337), **1** 1n.
from Dr E. G. Millar, **5** 89
Craven Ord MS., **3** 51, 52
Phillipps collection of drawings, **4** 223; **5** 104
Phillipps MSS., **5** 57, 59
Ranuzzi MSS., **4** 181
C. R. Rich's collection, **3** 129n.
Sherborne Cartulary, **5** 108
from Simonides, **4** x, 117
Souriani library, **3** 123n., 131
Stowe MSS., **3** 112n.
Taylor Oriental MSS. **4** 101n.
from Thorpe, **4** 7
MSS. stolen from Trinity College Library, **2** 39
autograph letters from Dawson Turner's collection, **4** 83
from Upcott sale, **3** 91
Reading Room, **4** 99
scholars' letters of introduction to Fenwick from, **5** 19
shelfmarks
of Joseph Barret MS., **3** 154
of Curzon MS., **4** 150n.
of former Phillipps MSS., **1** 1n.; **3** 41n., 78n.; **4** 161n., 162n.; **5** 57n., 59n., 61n., 87n., 118
of heraldic MS. by Thomas Glynn, **3** 169
of purchases from Simonides, **4** 117, 117n.; of other Simonides material, **4** 130n.
of Taylor Oriental MSS., **4** 101n.
of Dawson Turner autograph letters, **4** 83n.

Constantine Simonides, dealings with, **4** 116–17, 118, 128
staff mentioned (*for full entries see under individual names in index*)
Directors and Principal Librarians: Sir Henry Ellis; John Winter Jones; Sir Antony Panizzi; Edward Maunde Thompson
Dept. of Antiquities: Edward Hawkins; F. W. Madden
Dept. of Coins and Medals: William S. W. Vaux
Dept. of Manuscripts: Edward A. Bond; T. J. Brown; A. J. Collins; William Cureton; Godfrey Davis; R. E. W. Flower; Josiah Forshall; L. J. Gorton; John Holmes; Sir Frederic Madden; Eric G. Millar; T. C. Skeat; C. E. Wright
Dept. of Oriental Printed Books and Manuscripts: Jacob Leveen
Dept. of Printed Books: (John Winter Jones); (Sir Antony Panizzi); Thomas Yeates
Dept. of Prints and Drawings: A. E. Popham
Thorpe's views on the Museum as purchaser of his stock, **3** 84
Trustees, **4** 143
Phillipps as a Trustee, **2** 83–7; **4** 104–9, 144–5; **5** 8–9
Phillipps's suggestions for the Museum, **3** 65; **4** 106–9
Britton, John, **3** 7, 7n., 145, 169; **5** 57
Britwell sale, **5** 76
Brizzi, Serafino, **4** 226
Broadley, John, **3** 159
Broadway, Worcestershire
place mentioned, **2** 1, 2, 5, 19, 66, 73, 104, 110; **3** 16, 18, 70, 116; **4** 29, 32, 44, 60, 90, 214
Broadway Tower, **2** 2, 105n.; **3** 15, 16–18, 69; **4** 35, 88, 171
Broadway Tower vignette, **1** pl. IV, 12n., 38n., 39; **3** 114n., 120n.
Fish Inn, **3** 15

Buytewech, William Pietersz, **4** 226
Byland Abbey, Yorkshire, **5** 61
Bylandt, Charles Malcolm Ernest George van, Graaf, **5** 27–8
Bywater, Ingram, **5** 43, 67n.
Byzantium, Greek Emperors of, **3** 172

Cadby, John H. W., **4** 139, 194, 210
Caen, University of, **3** 165
Caerleon, Monmouthshire, monastery of, **4** 162; **5** 89
Caermarthenshire Monumental Inscriptions, **4** 158
Caesar, Sir Julius, **3** 82; **5** 57
Caesars—*Les douze Césars en Mignatures*, **5** 25
Caffin, Charles Smart, **2** 70
Cagliari, Paolo (Veronese), **4** 224, 226
Caird Trustees, **5** 109
Caird, Sir James, 1st Bart, **5** 107
Cairo
  Greek Patriarch at, **3** 176
  Old Cairo, **3** 176
  place mentioned, **3** 134
Calais, **3** 26, 51
Caley, John, **1** 15; **3** 59, 98–9, 161; **5** 57, 64
California, U.S.A., **4** 164
Calne, hundred of, Wiltshire, **3** 3–4
Cambrensis, Giraldus, **3** 94, 137; **5** 9, 82
Cambrian Archaeological Association, **4** 38; **5** 4
Cambridge Antiquarian Society, **2** 79
Cambridge University, **2** 37, 38, 47; **3** 63; **4** 170; **5** 42, 44
Cambridge University Reporter, **5** 44n.
Colleges
  Clare, **5** 44
  Corpus Christi, **5** 18
  Gonville and Caius, **3** 63; **4** 39
  Jesus, **2** 37
  King's, **3** 53; **4** 162n.
  Magdalene, **4** 39
  Peterhouse, **5** 45
  St John's, **4** 193
  Trinity: Halliwell matriculated at, **2** 37; Halliwell's theft of books

from, **2** xi, 39, 50, 79, 80, 84, 118; **3** 121; **4** 132; James Mayo of, **5** 45; William Whewell (Master), **4** 39
Fitzwilliam Museum, **5** 58n., 60
University Library
  Librarians: Henry Bradshaw, **4** 156; Francis Jenkinson, **4** 44–50, 61; John E. B. Mayor, **4** 93n.
  attempted negotiations with T. F. Fenwick, **5** 44–50
  cartularies in, **2** 38; **4** 138n.
  copies of *Catalogus Librorum Manuscriptorum*, **1** 8, 22, 23, 24, 33
  document on its history, **3** 105, 105n.
  Madden's collection of ballads in, **3** 112n.
  Phillipps MSS. bought at auction, **5** 59, 59n., 61, 89
  Phillipps transcribes MSS. in, **4** 39
Cambridge, Mass., Harvard University *see* Harvard University
Cambridgeshire, **3** 119
Cambron, Cistercian Abbey, **3** 23, 138, 146, 158
Camden Society, **2** 84n.; **4** 37
Campagnola, Domenico, **4** 226
Campbell, John, 1st Baron, **4** 81, 111
Campbell, John Frederick, 1st Earl of Cawdor, **1** 29; **3** 107n.; **4** 81
Canada, **4** 143; **5** 77, 77n., 87
Canning, Sir Stratford, 1st Viscount de Redcliffe, **3** 135; **4** 100, 100n.
Canonici MSS., **2** 38n.; **3** 50, 122n.
Canons, **5** 109
Canterbury, Kent
  Archbishop of, 1828–48 (William Howley), **3** 112, 113
  Christ Church, **3** 128n.
  place mentioned, **4** 201
Cape of Good Hope, **4** 73, 164
Caperonier, transcriber, **2** 39n.
Caracalla, monastery of, **3** 131, 132, 173
Carbonari, **4** 103
Cardew, John Haydon, **2** 106, 112, 114, 115; **5** 14, 21

11-2

Halliwell, James, relations with Phillipps (*cont.*)

J. C. Jeaffreson on Phillipps and Halliwell, **2** 118–19

scheme for reprinting *Catalogus Librorum Manuscriptorum*, **1** 15–16

thefts from Trinity College, Cambridge, **2** xi, 39, 50–2, 79–80, 118; **3** 121; **4** 132

Halliwell, Thomas, **2** 42, 43, 44, 45, 46, 47, 119

Hamilton, Alexander Hamilton-Douglas, 10th Duke of, **3** 63; **4** 26n., 96

Hamilton, William Alexander Anthony Archibald Douglas, 11th Duke of, **4** 95, 95n.

Hamilton, William Richard, **4** 99, 99n.

Hamilton Palace, Lanarkshire, **4** 95–6
sale, **5** 119

Hamm, University of, **3** 33

Hammond, W. H., **4** 180

Hampe, Karl, **5** 36n.

Hamper, William, **3** 164

Hampshire, county of, **3** 6, 6n.; **4** 112n.

Hand, J. T., **4** 205

Hanmer, Job Walden, **4** 180

Hanover, Germany, **4** 124

Hanrott, Philip Augustus, **4** 211

Harbin, George, **3** 56, 159, 169

Harding, Triphook and Lepard, **5** 116, 117

Harding, George Perfect, **3** viii

Hardy, Sir Thomas Duffus
biographical note, **3** 41n.
edits volume of *Monumenta Historica Britannica*, **3** 41
establishment of the Historical Manuscripts Commission, **4** 152n.
exchange of letters with Phillipps on, **4** 156–8
friend of J. C. Jeaffreson, **2** 118
Memoirs of Henry, Lord Langdale, **3** 99n.
quarrel with Sir Francis Palgrave, **2** 119

seeks reprint of *Catalogus Librorum Manuscriptorum*, **1** 15

supports idea of subscriptions to Bibliotheca Phillippica, **5** 15

visit to Thirlestaine, **2** 119

Hardyman, gardener at Middle Hill, **2** 22

Hare, Dr, **3** 63

Harleian MSS., **4** 72, 109, 180, 181, 185

Harley, Miss, **4** 72

Harley, Sir Robert, 1st Earl of Oxford, **1** 18; **4** 72, 170

Harlow cartulary, **4** 138

Harmsworth, Sir Leicester, **4** 137; **5** 98, 111

Harnack, Adolf von, **5** 40–1

Harper, Alfred, **4** 158

Harrasowitz, bookseller, **5** 59

Harris, James Rendel, **5** 66n.

Harris, John, **4** 140, 140n., 141

Harrison, Frederick, **4** xiv

Harrison, Joseph, **4** 58n.

Harrow School, Middlesex, **3** 53

Hartford Theological Seminary, Connecticut, **5** 18

Harte, Francis Bret, **4** 70

Hartland, afterwards Dixon-Hartland, Sir Frederick Dixon, Bart, **4** 68, 98–9, 98n.

Hartley, Leonard Lawrie, **5** 114, 118

Hartshorne, Charles Henry, **2** 36, 48; **3** 107 n.

Harvard University, Cambridge, Mass., **2** 87; **5** 102, 105, 109
Law School, **1** 24
Library, **1** 17, 24; **4** 14n., 29, 93–5; **5** xi, 59n., 62, 63n., 107n.
Houghton Library, **4** ix, 162n.
Peabody Museum of American Archaeology and Ethnology, **4** 150n.

Harward, John, **2** 5

Haseloff, Arthur, **5** 67n.

Haslewood, Joseph, **3** 113, 160

Hasselt, Louis van, **5** 27

Hasted, Edward, **4** 178

Hastings, Sir Charles, **4** 41n.

Paris, Matthew, **4** 149
Parish registers, **3** 64–5, 119; **4** 142, 157
Park, W., **4** xiv
Parke-Bernet Galleries, New York, **5** 107
Parker, Henry T., **4** 95
Parker, Mr, **3** 125
Parker, sale-room pseudonym of Sir T. Phillipps, **4** 75
Parkhurst, Fleetwood, **4** 177, 205
Parliament, Houses of, **4** 31, 43
 House of Commons, **3** 102n., 122
 House of Lords
  Library, **1** 31
  Select Committee, **3** 104–5
Parliamentary registers, **4** 136
Parmigianino (Girolamo Francesco Maria Mazzuoli), **4** 218–19
Parochial Collections for the County of Oxford, **3** 11–12
Parochial Libraries, **4** 43
On Parochial Registration of Baptisms, Marriages, etc., **3** 65n.
Parr, Samuel, **3** 144, 154
Patmos, monastery of St John, **3** 171
Patristic literature, **3** 170, 171, 172, 176; **5** 42, 47
Paul, Saint, **3** 174
Pauli, Reinhold, **5** 36n., 67n.
Paver, William, **3** 165; **4** 178
Payne and Foss
 account of the firm, **3** 43–5; **4** 1–3
 books sold to or obtained for Sir T. Phillipps, **3** 53, 55, 94, 149, 150, 153, 154, 155, 156, 158, 160, 161, 163, 164, 165, 166, 167, 168; **4** 3n., 154n., 176, 177, 180, 181, 184, 190; **5** 73
 commission on the execution of bids at auction, **3** 50, 76, 78, 99
 dealings with the Heber MSS., **3** 75, 76–8, 79, 80, 81
 dealings with Phillipps, **3** 96–7, 99, 109; **4** 1–3, 15, 18, 22
 mentioned, **3** 46; **4** 83; **5** 111
 purchases at the Meerman sale, **3** 26, 27
 sale of their MSS. at Sotheby's, **4** 79

Payne, John Thomas, **3** 27, 43, 44, 75, 77, 94; **4** ix, 1–3, 6, 15, 78, 79
Payne, Thomas, **3** 43
Payne, Thomas II, **3** 43, 44, 46, 55, 74
Peabody Museum of American Archaeology and Ethnology, Cambridge, Mass., **4** 150n.
Peak Forest Canal Company, Derbyshire, **2** 3
Pearson, Sir John, **5** 21
Peckover sale, **5** 99
Pecock, Reginald, Bishop of Chichester, **5** 64
Pedigrees from the Heraldic Visitation of Northumberland, 1815, **4** 112
Peel, Sir Robert, **3** 65–6, 101; **4** 12, 42
Peerages, **4** 20
Pelasgic letters, **4** 120
Pembroke College, Oxford, **3** 60, 62
Pembroke, William Marshal, 1st Earl of, Regent of England, **4** 163
Pembrokeshire, **2** 28; **4** 112, 135, 204
Peniarth, Merionethshire, **4** 158
Pennsylvania, University Library, **5** 115
Pentateuch, *see* Bible, Old Testament
Peover Hall, Cheshire, **4** 187
Pepys, Samuel, **5** 56
Pepysian Library, Magdalene College, Cambridge, **4** 39
Perceval, John, 1st Earl of Egmont, **4** 190
Percival MSS., **4** 181
Percy, Sir Algernon, 1st Baron Prudhoe and 4th Duke of Northumberland, **3** 123, 123n.; **4** 105
Percy, Hugh Algernon, 10th Duke of Northumberland, **4** 17n.; **5** 109
Perez de Guzman, Alonso, 7th Duke of Medina Sidonia, **4** 14n.; **5** 109
Periodicals, **5** 88
Perring, afterwards Molyneux, Elizabeth, **2** 12n.
Perring, Thomas, **2** 12n.
Perrins, Charles William Dyson, **5** 66n.
Persepolitan arrowhead characters, **4** 116
Pershore Abbey, Worcestershire, **4** 35

Souriani, monastery of, **3** 123 n., 131
Souter, Alexander, **5** 67 n.
South America, **4** 61, 62, 73; **5** 102, 109
Southampton, **3** 112
Southgate, J. W., **3** 147, 155, 158; **4** 186
South Sea Islands, **5** 88
Southwell, Edward, 21st Baron Clifford, **3** 164
Southwell, Sir Robert
 his papers and MSS., **3** 85, 85 n., 160, 164; **4** 208
 dispersal of Phillipps's collection of material from his library, **5** 54, 57, 63
Soviet Government, **5** 99
Sowdon of Babylone, The, **5** 61
Spain
 Academy, **4** 42
 Bibliotheca Nacional, **3** 95 n.
 conquest of Naples and Sicily by, **4** 136
 copies of MSS. made there for Lord Kingsborough, **4** 13
 Duke of Wellington's campaign in, **4** 201
 place mentioned, **4** 73
 Spanish MSS., **4** 14 n., 31, 201, 202; **5** 79, 109
 Spanish Romances, **3** 95–6; **5** 106
 Spanish tailors' pattern-book, **4** 165
Spanish America, **4** 141
Spanish and Portuguese Books in Middle Hill Library, 1852, **1** 40
Sparkes, Jared, *see next entry*
Sparks, Jared
 biographical note, **2** 87 n.
 correspondence with Phillipps, **3** 107 n.
 extracts from his diary, **4** 29–32
 invitation to Middle Hill, **2** 87
 opinion of Phillipps's library and hospitality, **4** 30, 32, 41–2, 94
 Phillipps's opinion of him, **4** 32
Sparrow, John, **4** xiv
Spegmenou, monastery of, **3** 174
Spelman, Sir Henry, **4** 83
Spencer, Hon. Captain, **2** pl. II

Spencer, George John, 2nd Earl, **1** 36; **3** 33, 74 n., 109, 113; **4** 16, 97
Speyer, of Basle, **3** 153
Spiess, bookseller of Cologne, **3** 21
Spicer, W. H., **3** 56–8
Spinks, John, **2** 31
Spinks, John, junior, **2** 31, 32, 33
Spira, Johannes de, **3** 94 n.; **5** 55
Spira, Vindelinus de, **3** 94 n.
Springfield, home of Lord Coventry, **3** 15
Staffa, Isle of, Argyllshire, **3** 63
Stafford, priory of St Thomas à Becket at, **3** 163
Staffordshire, **4** 91, 112 n.
Stageira, Island of, **4** 114
Stamford, Thomas Grey, 2nd Earl of, **3** 164, 166; **4** 208
Stamp Act, 1765, **5** 100
Stanhope, Philip Dormer, 4th Earl of Chesterfield, **2** 4–5, 7
Stanhope, Philip Henry, 5th Earl, **1** 7 n.
Stanton, William, **4** 187
Stanwick Hall, Yorkshire, **5** 97
Stapleton, Thomas, **1** 22, 33
State Paper Office, **3** 46; **4** 37, 156, 180. *See also* Public Record Office; Rolls Office; Tower Record Office
State papers, **3** 86, 88; **5** 57. *See also* Public records
Statistical Society of London, **4** 37 n.
Statius, Publius Papinius, **5** 25, 74
Stavelot, Benedictine abbey of, **4** 3, 3 n., 161, 180, 181; **5** 72
Stavroniketa, monastery of, **3** 173
Steele, Edward, **4** 185
Steele-Graves, Lady, **2** 89, 90; **4** 133
Steer, Francis William, **4** xiv, 26 n.
Steinfeld, Premonstratensian monastery, **3** 29, 146
Steinmetz, German editor of St Irenaeus, **4** 35
Stephenson, C. D., **4** 76 n.
Sterling, Sir Louis Saul, **5** 99, 100, 103, 106
Stern, Sir Albert, **4** 76 n.
Stettin, Germany, **5** 39